HOME DESIGN

This Journal Belongs to:

_____

If found please return to:

_____

_____

_____

This Home Design Journal is designed by Catherine Thrush.

Published by Urban Realms

Visit our website at www.urbanrealms.com

ISBN 978-0-9914788-5-9

Copyright 2015

Table of Contents

The Pros   3

Whole House Info   6

Bathrooms   9

    Remodel Checklist   10

    Master Bathroom   11

    Family Bathroom   23

    Guest Bathroom   35

Bedrooms   47

    Remodel Checklist   48

    Master Bedroom   49

    Bedroom 1   57

    Bedroom 2   65

    Bedroom 3   73

    Bedroom 4   81

    Bedroom 5   89

Eating Spaces   97

    Remodel Checklist   98

    Dining Room   99

    Kitchen   107

Living Spaces   123

    Remodel Checklist   124

    Den   125

    Family Room   133

    Home Theater   141

    Living Room   152

Work Spaces   160

    Remodel Checklist   161

    Home Office   162

    Laundry Room   173

    Walk-in Closet   183

The Pros

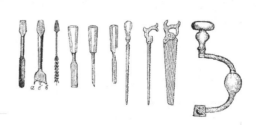

Contractor Company: _____

Contact Person: _____

Address: _____

_____

Phone: _____ Cell: _____

Handyman Company: _____

Contact Person: _____

Address: _____

_____

Phone: _____ Cell: _____

Electrical Company: _____

Contact Person: _____

Address: _____

_____

Phone: _____ Cell: _____

Plumbing Company: _____

Contact Person: _____

Address: _____

_____

Phone: _____ Cell: _____

Landscaping Company: _____

Contact Person: _____

Address: _____

_____

Phone: _____ Cell: _____

Other: _____

Contact Person: _____

Address: _____

_____

Phone: _____ Cell: _____

Other: _____

Contact Person: _____

Address: _____

_____

Phone: _____ Cell: _____

Other: _____

Contact Person: _____

Address: _____

_____

Phone: _____ Cell: _____

Other: _____

Contact Person: _____

Address: _____

_____

Phone: _____ Cell: _____

Other: _____

Contact Person: _____

Address: _____

_____

Phone: _____ Cell: _____

Other: _____

Contact Person: _____

Address: _____

_____

Phone: _____ Cell: _____

Other: _____

Contact Person: _____

Address: _____

_____

Phone: _____ Cell: _____

Other: _____

Contact Person: _____

Address: _____

_____

Phone: _____ Cell: _____

Other: _____

Contact Person: _____

Address: _____

_____

Phone: _____ Cell: _____

Other: _____

Contact Person: _____

Address: _____

_____

Phone: _____ Cell: _____

Whole House Info

Attic Fan

Manufacturer: _____

Style/Model Info: _____

_____

Website: _____

Purchased at: _____

Installed by: _____

Air Conditioner

Last Serviced On

Manufacturer: _____   _____

Style/Model Info: _____   _____

_____   _____

Website: _____   _____

Purchased at: _____   _____

Installed by: _____   _____

Electrical Panel

Notes

Where it is located: _____

Type of panel: _____

_____

Power Company: _____

Circuits left: _____

Purchased at: _____

Electrician: _____

Furnace

Manufacturer: _____

Style/Model Info: _____   BTUs: _____

_____   Filter Size _____

Gas or Electric: _____   Changed Filter On

Service company contact info: _____

Website: _____   _____

Purchased at: _____   _____

Installed by: _____   _____

Gas

Meter location: _____   Notes

Shut off location: _____

_____

Gas company contact info: _____

Gas appliances: _____

Gas provider: _____

Installed by: _____

Water

Shut off location: _____   Notes

_____

Sprinkler controller location: _____

_____

Water provider: _____

Plumber: _____

Water Heater

Manufacturer: _____

Style/Model Info: _____

_____

Website: _____

Purchased at: _____

Installed by: _____

_____

_____

_____

_____

_____

_____

Water Softener

Manufacturer: _____

Style/Model Info: _____

_____

Service company contact info: _____

Website: _____

Purchased at: _____

Installed by: _____

Last Serviced On

_____

_____

_____

_____

_____

_____

_____

Manufacturer: _____

Style/Model Info: _____

_____

Service company contact info: _____

Website: _____

Purchased at: _____

Installed by: _____

Notes

Bathrooms

Bath Remodel Checklist (Check those that will be changed)

Item	Master Bath	Family Bath	Guest Bath
Door			
Drywall			
Electrical			
Electrical outlets			
Fan			
GFI outlet			
Lighting			
Switches			
Timers			
Flooring			
Mirror/Storage			
Plaster			
Plumbing			
Drains			
Faucets			
Pipes			
Shower			
Sink			
Toilet			
Tub			
Tile			
Trim			
Base Moulding			
Crown Moulding			
Door/Window			
Vanity			
Vanity Top			
Wall Covering			
Window			
Window Covering			

Master Bathroom

Fan

Manufacturer: _____

Style/Model Info: _____

_____

Website: _____

Purchased at: _____

Installed by: _____

Specs:

Voltage:_____

Light: yes   no

Bulb type: _____

Wattage: _____

Flooring

Material: _____

Manufacturer: _____

Style/Model Info: _____

_____

Design Pattern: _____

Website: _____

Purchased at: _____

Installed by: _____

Area

L _____ X

W _____

= _____

Add an extra 10% =

_____

Lighting Fixture 1

Manufacturer: _____

Style/Model Info: _____

_____

Website: _____

Purchased at: _____

Installed by: _____

Bulbs

Wattage _____

Type _____

From_____

Changed_____

Lighting Fixture 2

Manufacturer: _____

Style/Model Info: _____

_____

Website: _____

Purchased at: _____

Installed by: _____

Bulbs

Wattage _____

Type _____

From_____

Changed_____

Mirror / Medicine Cabinet

Manufacturer: _____

Style/Model Info: _____

_____

Website: _____

Purchased at: _____

Installed by: _____

Dimensions

L _____

W_____

Type _____

Shape

_____

Material

_____

Plumbing Fixtures

Sink

Material: _____

Manufacturer: _____

Style/Model Info: _____

_____

Website: _____

Purchased at: _____

Installed by: _____

Dimensions

L _____

W_____

Faucet Center _____

Faucet Holes _____

Material

_____

Sink Faucet

Manufacturer: _____

Style/Model Info: _____

_____

Finish: _____

Website: _____

Purchased at: _____

Installed by: _____

Specifications

of Holes _____

Spread _____

Mount _____

Finish _____

Toilet

Manufacturer: _____

Style/Model Info: _____

_____

Website: _____

Purchased at: _____

Installed by: _____

Specifications

Rough in _____

Configuration

_____

Mount _____

Flush type

_____

Tub / Shower

Material: _____

Manufacturer: _____

Style/Model Info: _____

_____

Website: _____

Purchased at: _____

Installed by: _____

Dimensions

L _____

W_____

Type _____

Shape

_____

Material

_____

Tub / Shower faucet

Manufacturer: _____

Style/Model Info: _____

_____

Height of shower head: _____

Website: _____

Purchased at: _____

Installed by: _____

Specifications

# of Handles _____

Valve type

_____

Handle style

_____

Finish

_____

Tile

Accent Tile 1

Manufacturer: _____

Style/Model Info: _____

_____

Pattern: _____

Website: _____

Purchased at: _____

Installed by:_____

Dimensions

L _____

W_____

Thickness _____

Type_____

Material

_____

Accent Tile 2

Manufacturer: _____

Style/Model Info: _____

_____

Pattern: _____

Website: _____

Purchased at: _____

Installed by: _____

Dimensions

L _____

W_____

Thickness _____

Type _____

Material

_____

Main Tile

Manufacturer: _____

Style/Model Info: _____

_____

Pattern: _____

Website: _____

Purchased at: _____

Installed by: _____

Dimensions

L _____

W _____

Thickness _____

Type _____

Material

_____

≡ Trim Work

Crown Molding

Manufacturer: _____

Style/Model Info: _____

_____

Paint / Stain: _____

Website: _____

Purchased at: _____

Installed by: _____

Linear Footage

Wall 1 _____

Wall 2 _____

Wall 3 _____

Wall 4 _____

Total _____

Floor Molding / Tile Base

Manufacturer: _____

Style/Model Info: _____

_____

Paint / Stain: _____

Website: _____

Purchased at: _____

Installed by: _____

Linear Footage

Wall 1 _____

Wall 2 _____

Wall 3 _____

Wall 4 _____

Total _____

Window / Door Trim

Manufacturer: _____

Style/Model Info: _____

_____

Paint / Stain: _____

Website: _____

Purchased at: _____

Installed by: _____

Linear Footage

Wall 1 _____

Wall 2 _____

Wall 3 _____

Wall 4 _____

Total _____

Vanity

Manufacturer: _____

Style/Model Info: _____

_____

Paint or Stain: _____

Website: _____

Purchased at: _____

Installed by: _____

Body Dimensions

L _____

W_____

H _____

Material

_____

Vanity Top

Material: _____

Manufacturer: _____

Style/Model Info: _____

_____

Website: _____

Purchased at: _____

Installed by: _____

Top Dimensions

L _____

W_____

Thickness _____

Wall Covering / Paint 1

Manufacturer: _____

Style/Model Info: _____

_____

Website: _____

Purchased at: _____

Installed by:_____

Area

L _____ X

W _____

= _____

Add an extra 10% =

_____

Wall Covering / Paint 2

Manufacturer: _____

Style/Model Info: _____

_____

Website: _____

Purchased at: _____

Installed by:_____

Area

L _____ X

W _____

= _____

Add an extra 10% =

_____

Wall Mounted Fixtures

Towel Bars

Manufacturer: _____

Style/Model Info: _____

_____

Toilet Paper Holders

Manufacturer: _____

Style/Model Info: _____

_____

Notes:

Accessories

_____

_____

_____

_____

_____

_____

_____

_____

_____

_____

_____

_____

_____

_____

Staple Fabric Swatches / Color Chips Here

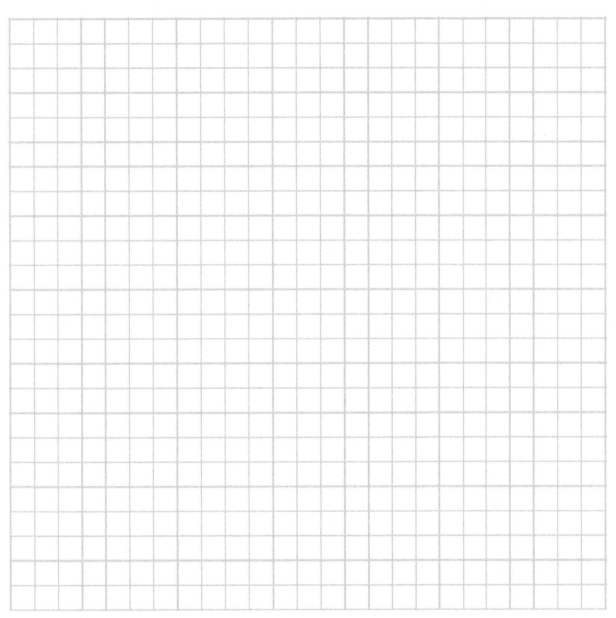

Master Bath Floor Plan

Room Dimensions _____   Window Dimensions_____

Vanity Dimensions _____ Tub/Shower Dimensions_____

Toilet Dimensions_____   Other _____

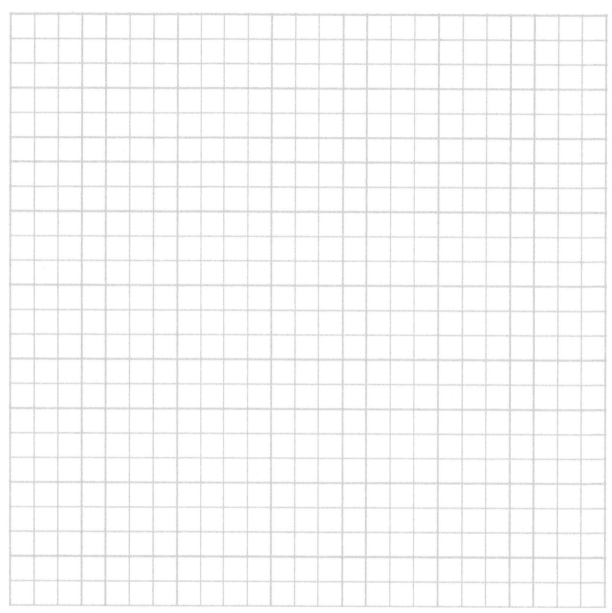

Master Bath Main Wall Elevation

Wall Dimensions _____ Window Dimensions_____

Vanity Dimensions _____ Tub/Shower Dimensions_____

Sink Dimensions_____ Faucet Size_____

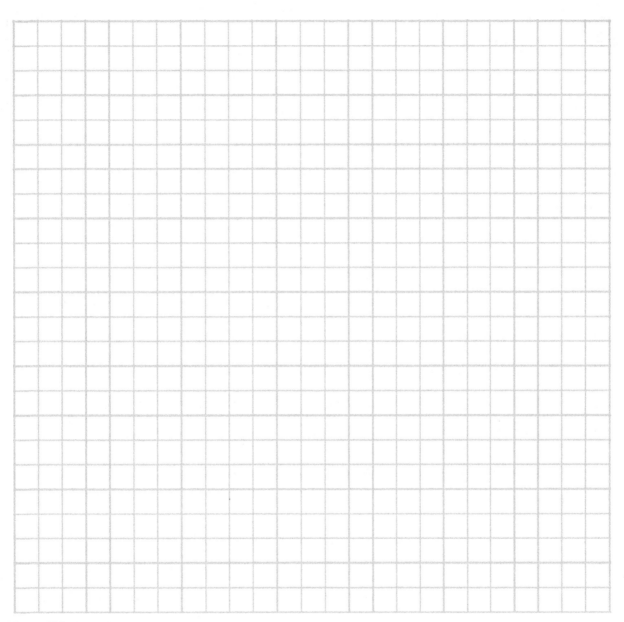

Tile Planner

Wall Dimensions _____   Vanity Dimensions _____

Tub/Shower Dimensions_____   Tile Dimensions_____

Accent Tile Size_____

Ideas & Inspiration

Style cues :

My Wish List :

Notes !

Color Swatches :

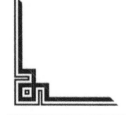

Family Bathroom

Fan

Manufacturer: _____

Style/Model Info: _____

_____

Website: _____

Purchased at: _____

Installed by: _____

Specs:

Voltage: _____

Light: yes   no

Bulb type: _____

Wattage: _____

Flooring

Material: _____

Manufacturer: _____

Style/Model Info: _____

_____

Design Pattern: _____

Website: _____

Purchased at: _____

Installed by: _____

Area

L _____ X

W _____

= _____

Add an extra 10% =

_____

Lighting Fixture 1

Manufacturer: _____

Style/Model Info: _____

_____

Website: _____

Purchased at: _____

Installed by: _____

Bulbs

Wattage _____

Type _____

From_____

Changed_____

Lighting Fixture 2

Manufacturer: _____

Style/Model Info: _____

_____

Website: _____

Purchased at: _____

Installed by: _____

Bulbs

Wattage _____

Type _____

From_____

Changed_____

Mirror / Medicine Cabinet

Manufacturer: _____

Style/Model Info: _____

_____

Website: _____

Purchased at: _____

Installed by: _____

Dimensions

L _____

W_____

Type _____

Shape
_____

Material
_____

Plumbing Fixtures

Sink

Material: _____

Manufacturer: _____

Style/Model Info: _____

_____

Website: _____

Purchased at: _____

Installed by: _____

Dimensions

L _____

W_____

Faucet Center _____

Faucet Holes _____

Material _____

Sink Faucet

Manufacturer: _____

Style/Model Info: _____

_____

Finish: _____

Website: _____

Purchased at: _____

Installed by: _____

Specifications

# of Holes _____

Spread _____

Mount _____

Finish _____

Toilet

Manufacturer: _____

Style/Model Info: _____

_____

Website: _____

Purchased at: _____

Installed by: _____

Specifications

Rough in _____

Configuration

_____

Mount _____

Flush type

_____

Tub / Shower

Material: _____

Manufacturer: _____

Style/Model Info: _____

_____

Website: _____

Purchased at: _____

Installed by: _____

Dimensions

L _____

W_____

Type _____

Shape

_____

Material

_____

Tub / Shower faucet

Manufacturer: _____

Style/Model Info: _____

_____

Height of shower head: _____

Website: _____

Purchased at: _____

Installed by: _____

Specifications

of Handles _____

Valve type

_____

Handle style

_____

Finish

_____

❖ Tile

Accent Tile 1

Manufacturer: _____

Style/Model Info: _____

_____

Pattern: _____

Website: _____

Purchased at: _____

Installed by: _____

Dimensions

L _____

W_____

Thickness _____

Type_____

Material

_____

Accent Tile 2

Manufacturer: _____

Style/Model Info: _____

_____

Pattern: _____

Website: _____

Purchased at: _____

Installed by: _____

Dimensions

L _____

W_____

Thickness _____

Type _____

Material

_____

Main Tile

Manufacturer: _____

Style/Model Info: _____

_____

Pattern: _____

Website: _____

Purchased at: _____

Installed by: _____

Dimensions

L _____

W_____

Thickness _____

Type _____

Material

_____

▦ Trim Work

Crown Molding

Manufacturer: _____

Style/Model Info: _____

_____

Paint / Stain: _____

Website: _____

Purchased at: _____

Installed by: _____

Linear Footage

Wall 1 _____

Wall 2 _____

Wall 3 _____

Wall 4 _____

Total _____

Floor Molding / Tile Base

Manufacturer: _____

Style/Model Info: _____

_____

Paint / Stain: _____

Website: _____

Purchased at: _____

Installed by: _____

Linear Footage

Wall 1 _____

Wall 2 _____

Wall 3 _____

Wall 4 _____

Total _____

Window / Door Trim

Manufacturer: _____

Style/Model Info: _____

_____

Paint / Stain: _____

Website: _____

Purchased at: _____

Installed by: _____

Linear Footage

Wall 1 _____

Wall 2 _____

Wall 3 _____

Wall 4 _____

Total _____

Vanity

Manufacturer: _____

Style/Model Info: _____

_____

Paint or Stain: _____

Website: _____

Purchased at: _____

Installed by: _____

Body Dimensions

L _____

W_____

H _____

Material

_____

Vanity Top

Material: _____

Manufacturer: _____

Style/Model Info: _____

_____

Website: _____

Purchased at: _____

Installed by: _____

Top Dimensions

L _____

W_____

Thickness _____

Wall Covering / Paint 1

Manufacturer: _____

Style/Model Info: _____

_____

Website: _____

Purchased at: _____

Installed by:_____

Area

L _____ X

W _____

= _____

Add an extra 10% =

_____

Wall Covering / Paint 2

Manufacturer: _____

Style/Model Info: _____

_____

Website: _____

Purchased at: _____

Installed by:_____

Area

L _____ X

W _____

= _____

Add an extra 10% =

_____

Wall Mounted Fixtures

Towel Bars

Manufacturer: _____

Style/Model Info: _____

_____

Toilet Paper Holders

Manufacturer: _____

Style/Model Info: _____

_____

Notes:

Accessories

_____

_____

_____

_____

_____

_____

_____

_____

_____

_____

_____

_____

_____

Staple Fabric Swatches / Color Chips Here

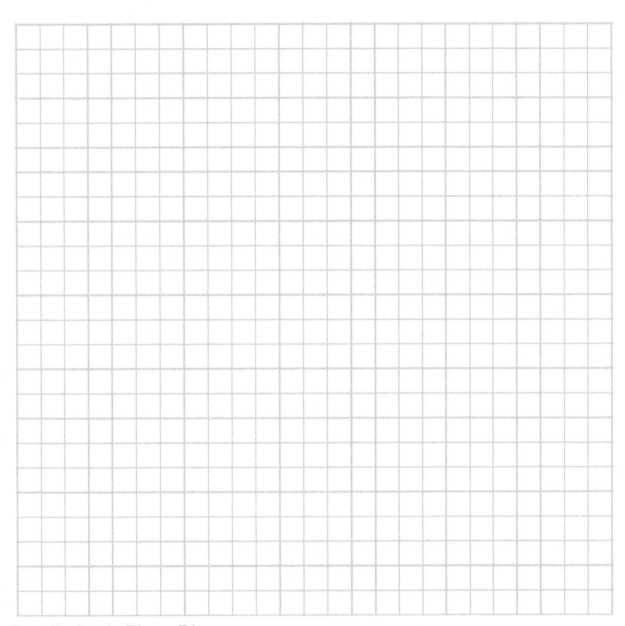

Family Bath Floor Plan

Room Dimensions _____   Window Dimensions_____

Vanity Dimensions _____   Tub/Shower Dimensions_____

Toilet Dimensions_____   Other _____

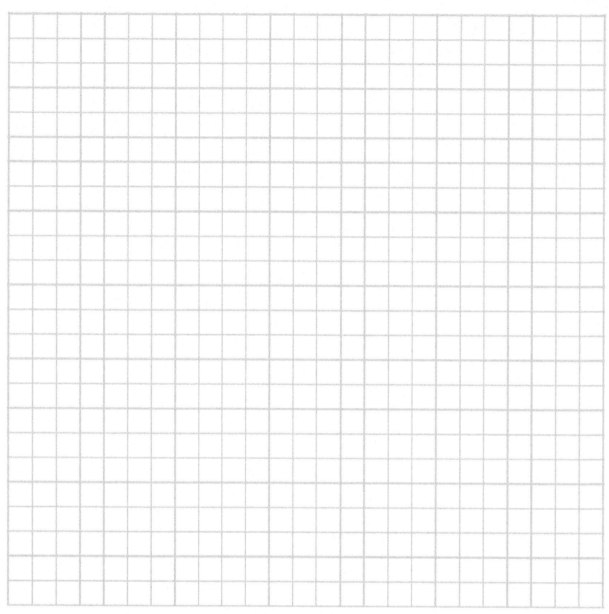

Family Bath Main Wall Elevation

Wall Dimensions _____   Window Dimensions_____

Vanity Dimensions _____   Tub/Shower Dimensions_____

Sink Dimensions_____   Faucet Size_____

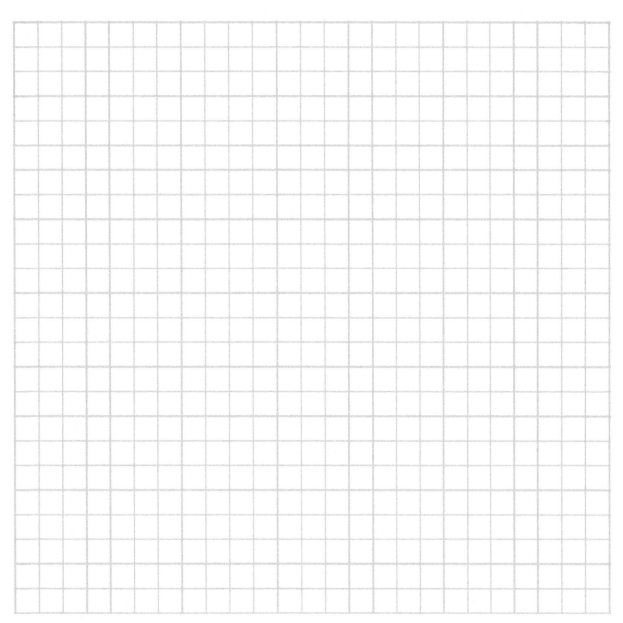

Tile Planner

Wall Dimensions _____   Vanity Dimensions _____

Tub/Shower Dimensions_____   Tile Dimensions_____

Accent Tile Size_____

Ideas & Inspiration

Guest Bathroom

Fan

Manufacturer: _____

Style/Model Info: _____

_____

Website: _____

Purchased at: _____

Installed by: _____

Specs:

Voltage: _____

Light: yes   no

Bulb type: _____

Wattage: _____

Flooring

Material: _____

Manufacturer: _____

Style/Model Info: _____

_____

Design Pattern: _____

Website: _____

Purchased at: _____

Installed by: _____

Area

L _____ X

W _____

= _____

Add an extra 10% =

_____

Lighting Fixture 1

Manufacturer: _____

Style/Model Info: _____

_____

Website: _____

Purchased at: _____

Installed by: _____

Bulbs

Wattage _____

Type _____

From _____

Changed _____

Lighting Fixture 2

Manufacturer: _____

Style/Model Info: _____

_____

Website: _____

Purchased at: _____

Installed by: _____

Bulbs

Wattage _____

Type _____

From_____

Changed_____

Mirror / Medicine Cabinet

Manufacturer: _____

Style/Model Info: _____

_____

Website: _____

Purchased at: _____

Installed by: _____

Dimensions

L _____

W_____

Type _____

Shape

_____

Material

_____

Plumbing Fixtures

Sink

Material: _____

Manufacturer: _____

Style/Model Info: _____

_____

Website: _____

Purchased at: _____

Installed by: _____

Dimensions

L _____

W_____

Faucet Center

_____

Faucet Holes

_____

Material

_____

Sink Faucet

Manufacturer: _____

Style/Model Info: _____

_____

Finish: _____

Website: _____

Purchased at: _____

Installed by: _____

Specifications

of Holes _____

Spread _____

Mount _____

Finish _____

Toilet

Manufacturer: _____

Style/Model Info: _____

_____

Website: _____

Purchased at: _____

Installed by: _____

Specifications

Rough in _____

Configuration

_____

Mount _____

Flush type

_____

Tub / Shower

Material: _____

Manufacturer: _____

Style/Model Info: _____

_____

Website: _____

Purchased at: _____

Installed by: _____

Dimensions

L _____

W_____

Type _____

Shape

_____

Material

_____

Tub / Shower faucet

Manufacturer: _____

Style/Model Info: _____

_____

Height of shower head: _____

Website: _____

Purchased at: _____

Installed by: _____

Specifications

of Handles _____

Valve type

_____

Handle style

_____

Finish

_____

❋ Tile

Accent Tile 1

Manufacturer: _____

Style/Model Info: _____

_____

Pattern: _____

Website: _____

Purchased at: _____

Installed by: _____

Dimensions

L _____

W_____

Thickness _____

Type_____

Material

_____

Accent Tile 2

Manufacturer: _____

Style/Model Info: _____

_____

Pattern: _____

Website: _____

Purchased at: _____

Installed by: _____

Dimensions

L _____

W_____

Thickness _____

Type _____

Material

_____

Main Tile

Manufacturer: _____

Style/Model Info: _____

_____

Pattern: _____

Website: _____

Purchased at: _____

Installed by: _____

Dimensions

L _____

W_____

Thickness _____

Type _____

Material

_____

Trim Work

Crown Molding

Manufacturer: _____

Style/Model Info: _____

_____

Paint / Stain: _____

Website: _____

Purchased at: _____

Installed by: _____

Linear Footage

Wall 1 _____

Wall 2 _____

Wall 3 _____

Wall 4 _____

Total _____

Floor Molding / Tile Base

Manufacturer: _____

Style/Model Info: _____

_____

Paint / Stain: _____

Website: _____

Purchased at: _____

Installed by: _____

Linear Footage

Wall 1 _____

Wall 2 _____

Wall 3 _____

Wall 4 _____

Total _____

Window / Door Trim

Manufacturer: _____

Style/Model Info: _____

_____

Paint / Stain: _____

Website: _____

Purchased at: _____

Installed by: _____

Linear Footage

Wall 1 _____

Wall 2 _____

Wall 3 _____

Wall 4 _____

Total _____

Vanity

Manufacturer: _____

Style/Model Info: _____

_____

Paint or Stain: _____

Website: _____

Purchased at: _____

Installed by: _____

Body Dimensions

L _____

W _____

H _____

Material

_____

Vanity Top

Material: _____

Manufacturer: _____

Style/Model Info: _____

_____

Website: _____

Purchased at: _____

Installed by: _____

Top Dimensions

L _____

W _____

Thickness _____

Wall Covering / Paint 1

Manufacturer: _____

Style/Model Info: _____

_____

Website: _____

Purchased at: _____

Installed by: _____

Area

L _____ X

W _____

= _____

Add an extra 10% =

_____

Wall Covering / Paint 2

Manufacturer: _____

Style/Model Info: _____

_____

Website: _____

Purchased at: _____

Installed by: _____

Area

L _____ X

W _____

= _____

Add an extra 10% =

_____

Wall Mounted Fixtures

Notes:

Towel Bars

Manufacturer: _____

Style/Model Info: _____

_____

Toilet Paper Holders

Manufacturer: _____

Style/Model Info: _____

_____

Accessories

_____

_____

_____

_____

_____

_____

_____

_____

_____

_____

_____

_____

_____

_____

Staple Fabric Swatches / Color Chips Here

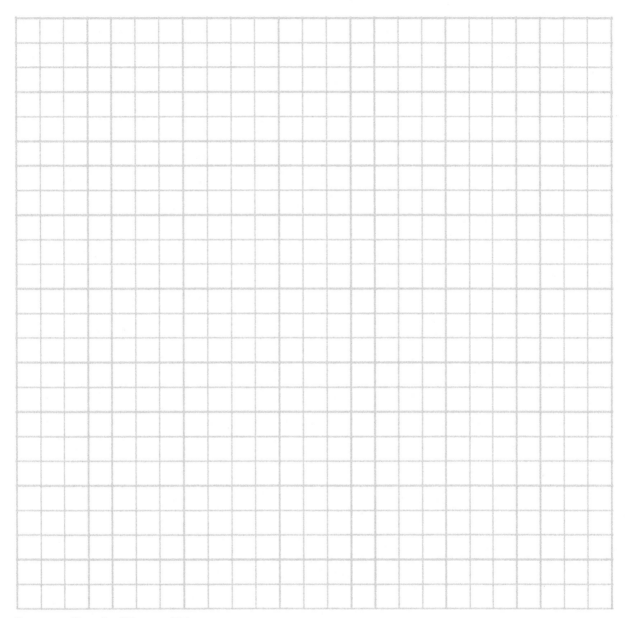

Guest Bath Floor Plan

Room Dimensions _____ Window Dimensions_____

Vanity Dimensions _____ Tub/Shower Dimensions_____

Toilet Dimensions_____ Other _____

Guest Bath Main Wall Elevation

Wall Dimensions _____   Window Dimensions_____

Vanity Dimensions _____ Tub/Shower Dimensions_____

Sink Dimensions_____ Faucet Size_____

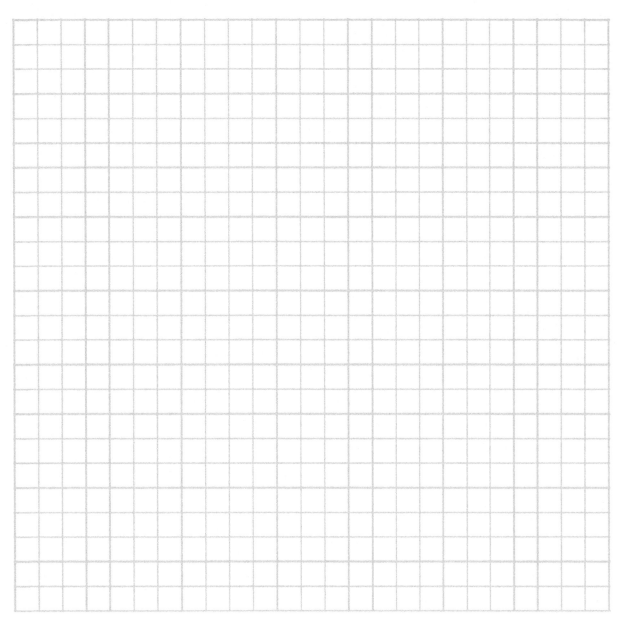

Tile Planner

Wall Dimensions _____ Vanity Dimensions _____

Tub/Shower Dimensions_____ Tile Dimensions_____

Accent Tile Size_____

Ideas & Inspiration

Bedrooms

Bedroom Remodel Checklist (Check those that will be changed)

Item	Master	1	2	3	4	5
Door						
Drywall						
Electrical						
Electrical outlets						
Fan						
Lighting						
Switches						
Dimers						
Flooring						
Storage						
Plaster						
Tile						
Trim						
Base Moulding						
Crown Moulding						
Door/Window						
Wall Covering						
Window						
Window Covering						

Master Bedroom

Flooring

Material: _____

Manufacturer: _____

Style/Model Info: _____

_____

Design Pattern: _____

Website: _____

Purchased at: _____

Installed by: _____

Area

L _____ X

W _____

= _____

Add an extra 10% =

_____

Lighting Fixture 1

Manufacturer: _____

Style/Model Info: _____

_____

Website: _____

Purchased at: _____

Installed by: _____

Bulbs

Wattage _____

Type _____

From_____

Changed_____

Lighting Fixture 2

Manufacturer: _____

Style/Model Info: _____

_____

Website: _____

Purchased at: _____

Installed by: _____

Bulbs

Wattage _____

Type _____

From_____

Changed_____

Lighting Fixture 3

Manufacturer: _____

Style/Model Info: _____

_____

Website: _____

Purchased at: _____

Installed by: _____

Bulbs

Wattage _____

Type _____

From_____

Changed_____

Trim Work

Crown Molding

Manufacturer: _____

Style/Model Info: _____

_____

Paint / Stain: _____

Website: _____

Purchased at: _____

Installed by: _____

Linear Footage

Wall 1 _____

Wall 2 _____

Wall 3 _____

Wall 4 _____

Total _____

Floor Molding / Tile Base

Manufacturer: _____

Style/Model Info: _____

_____

Paint / Stain: _____

Website: _____

Purchased at: _____

Installed by: _____

Linear Footage

Wall 1 _____

Wall 2 _____

Wall 3 _____

Wall 4 _____

Total _____

Window / Door Trim

Manufacturer: _____

Style/Model Info: _____

_____

Paint / Stain: _____

Website: _____

Purchased at: _____

Installed by: _____

Linear Footage

Wall 1 _____

Wall 2 _____

Wall 3 _____

Wall 4 _____

Total _____

Wall Covering / Paint 1

Manufacturer: _____

Color: _____

Style/Model Info: _____

_____

Website: _____

Purchased at: _____

Installed by: _____

Area

L _____ X

W _____

= _____

Add an extra 10% =

_____

Wall Covering / Paint 2

Manufacturer: _____

Color: _____

Style/Model Info: _____

_____

Website: _____

Purchased at: _____

Installed by: _____

Area

L _____ X

W _____

= _____

Add an extra 10% =

_____

⊞ Windows

Manufacturer: _____

Style/Model Info: _____

_____

Website: _____

Purchased at: _____

Installed by: _____

Dimensions

W_____

H _____

Type

_____

Material

_____

▐ Window Coverings 1

Manufacturer: _____

Style/Model Info: _____

_____

Rod or Holder: _____

_____

Website: _____

Purchased at: _____

Installed by: _____

Dimensions

L _____

W_____

H _____

Type

_____

Material

_____

Window Coverings 2

Manufacturer: _____

Style/Model Info: _____

_____

Rod or Holder: _____

_____

Website: _____

Purchased at: _____

Installed by: _____

Dimensions

L _____

W_____

H _____

Type

_____

Material

_____

Accessories

_____

_____

_____

_____

_____

_____

_____

_____

_____

_____

_____

_____

_____

_____

Staple Fabric Swatches / Color Chips Here

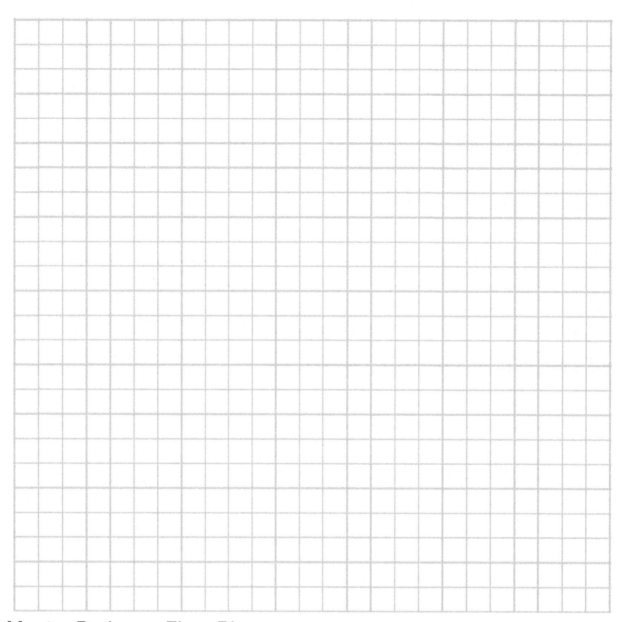

Master Bedroom Floor Plan

Room Dimensions _____   Window Dimensions_____

Door Dimensions _____   Bed Dimensions _____

Other _____

Master Bedroom Main Wall Elevation

Wall Dimensions _____   Window Dimensions_____

Bed Dimensions _____   Dresser Dimensions_____

Other _____

Ideas & Inspiration

Bedroom 1 _____

Flooring

Material: _____

Manufacturer: _____

Style/Model Info: _____

_____

Design Pattern: _____

Website: _____

Purchased at: _____

Installed by: _____

Area

L _____ X

W _____

= _____

Add an extra 10% =

_____

Lighting Fixture 1

Manufacturer: _____

Style/Model Info: _____

_____

Website: _____

Purchased at: _____

Installed by: _____

Bulbs

Wattage _____

Type _____

From _____

Changed _____

Lighting Fixture 2

Manufacturer: _____

Style/Model Info: _____

_____

Website: _____

Purchased at: _____

Installed by: _____

Bulbs

Wattage _____

Type _____

From _____

Changed _____

Lighting Fixture 3

Manufacturer: _____

Style/Model Info: _____

_____

Website: _____

Purchased at: _____

Installed by: _____

Bulbs .

Wattage _____

Type _____

From_____

Changed_____

Trim Work

Crown Molding

Manufacturer: _____

Style/Model Info: _____

_____

Paint / Stain: _____

Website: _____

Purchased at: _____

Installed by: _____

Linear Footage

Wall 1 _____

Wall 2 _____

Wall 3 _____

Wall 4 _____

Total _____

Floor Molding / Tile Base

Manufacturer: _____

Style/Model Info: _____

_____

Paint / Stain: _____

Website: _____

Purchased at: _____

Installed by: _____

Linear Footage

Wall 1 _____

Wall 2 _____

Wall 3 _____

Wall 4 _____

Total _____

Window / Door Trim

Manufacturer: _____

Style/Model Info: _____

_____

Paint / Stain: _____

Website: _____

Purchased at: _____

Installed by: _____

Linear Footage

Wall 1 _____

Wall 2 _____

Wall 3 _____

Wall 4 _____

Total _____

Wall Covering / Paint 1

Manufacturer: _____

Color: _____

Style/Model Info: _____

_____

Website: _____

Purchased at: _____

Installed by: _____

Area

L _____ X

W _____

= _____

Add an extra 10% =

_____

Wall Covering / Paint 2

Manufacturer: _____

Color: _____

Style/Model Info: _____

_____

Website: _____

Purchased at: _____

Installed by: _____

Area

L _____ X

W _____

= _____

Add an extra 10% =

_____

Bedroom 1

⊞ Windows

Manufacturer: _____

Style/Model Info: _____

_____

Website: _____

Purchased at: _____

Installed by: _____

Dimensions

W_____

H _____

Type
_____

Material
_____

▐▌ Window Coverings 1

Manufacturer: _____

Style/Model Info: _____

_____

Rod or Holder: _____

_____

Website: _____

Purchased at: _____

Installed by: _____

Dimensions

L _____

W_____

H _____

Type
_____

Material
_____

Window Coverings 2

Manufacturer: _____

Style/Model Info: _____

_____

Rod or Holder: _____

_____

Website: _____

Purchased at: _____

Installed by: _____

Dimensions

L _____

W_____

H _____

Type
_____

Material
_____

Accessories

Staple Fabric Swatches / Color Chips Here

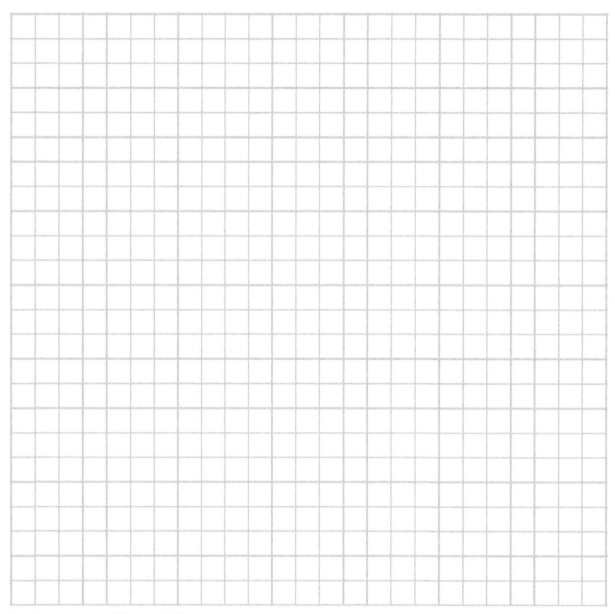

Bedroom 1 Floor Plan

Room Dimensions _____   Window Dimensions_____

Door Dimensions _____   Bed Dimensions _____

Other _____

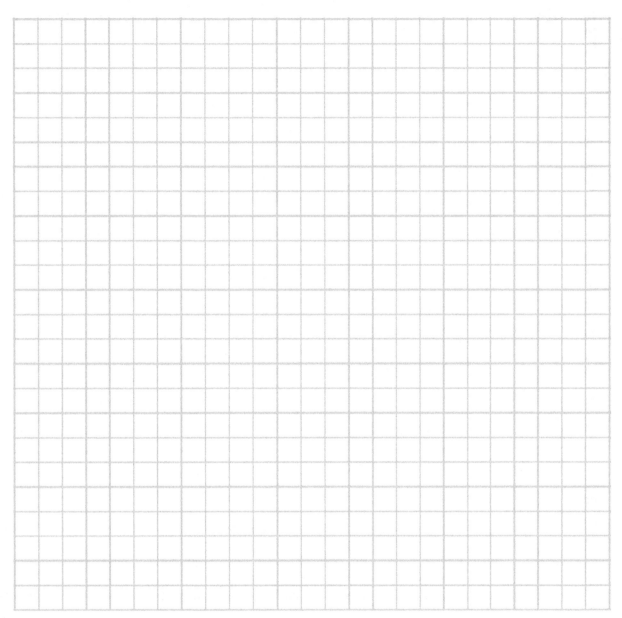

Bedroom 1 Main Wall Elevation

Wall Dimensions _____   Window Dimensions_____

Bed Dimensions _____   Dresser Dimensions_____

Other _____

Ideas & Inspiration

Bedroom 2 _____

Flooring

Material: _____

Manufacturer: _____

Style/Model Info: _____

_____

Design Pattern: _____

Website: _____

Purchased at: _____

Installed by: _____

Area

L _____ X

W _____

= _____

Add an extra 10% =

_____

Lighting Fixture 1

Manufacturer: _____

Style/Model Info: _____

_____

Website: _____

Purchased at: _____

Installed by: _____

Bulbs

Wattage _____

Type _____

From _____

Changed _____

Lighting Fixture 2

Manufacturer: _____

Style/Model Info: _____

_____

Website: _____

Purchased at: _____

Installed by: _____

Bulbs

Wattage _____

Type _____

From _____

Changed _____

Lighting Fixture 3

Manufacturer: _____

Style/Model Info: _____

_____

Website: _____

Purchased at: _____

Installed by: _____

Bulbs

Wattage _____

Type _____

From _____

Changed _____

Trim Work

Crown Molding

Manufacturer: _____

Style/Model Info: _____

_____

Paint / Stain: _____

Website: _____

Purchased at: _____

Installed by: _____

Linear Footage

Wall 1 _____

Wall 2 _____

Wall 3 _____

Wall 4 _____

Total _____

Floor Molding / Tile Base

Manufacturer: _____

Style/Model Info: _____

_____

Paint / Stain: _____

Website: _____

Purchased at: _____

Installed by: _____

Linear Footage

Wall 1 _____

Wall 2 _____

Wall 3 _____

Wall 4 _____

Total _____

Window / Door Trim

Manufacturer: _____

Style/Model Info: _____

_____

Paint / Stain: _____

Website: _____

Purchased at: _____

Installed by: _____

Linear Footage

Wall 1 _____

Wall 2 _____

Wall 3 _____

Wall 4 _____

Total _____

Wall Covering / Paint 1

Manufacturer: _____

Color: _____

Style/Model Info: _____

_____

Website: _____

Purchased at: _____

Installed by:_____

Area

L _____ X

W _____

= _____

Add an extra 10% =

_____

Wall Covering / Paint 2

Manufacturer: _____

Color: _____

Style/Model Info: _____

_____

Website: _____

Purchased at: _____

Installed by:_____

Area

L _____ X

W _____

= _____

Add an extra 10% =

_____

Bedroom 2

⊞ Windows

Manufacturer: _____

Style/Model Info: _____

_____

Website: _____

Purchased at: _____

Installed by: _____

Dimensions

W_____

H_____

Type

_____

Material

_____

▌▌ Window Coverings 1

Manufacturer: _____

Style/Model Info: _____

_____

Rod or Holder: _____

_____

Website: _____

Purchased at: _____

Installed by: _____

Dimensions

L_____

W_____

H_____

Type

_____

Material

_____

Window Coverings 2

Manufacturer: _____

Style/Model Info: _____

_____

Rod or Holder: _____

_____

Website: _____

Purchased at: _____

Installed by: _____

Dimensions

L_____

W_____

H_____

Type

_____

Material

_____

Accessories

_____

_____

_____

_____

_____

_____

_____

_____

_____

_____

_____

_____

_____

_____

Staple Fabric Swatches / Color Chips Here

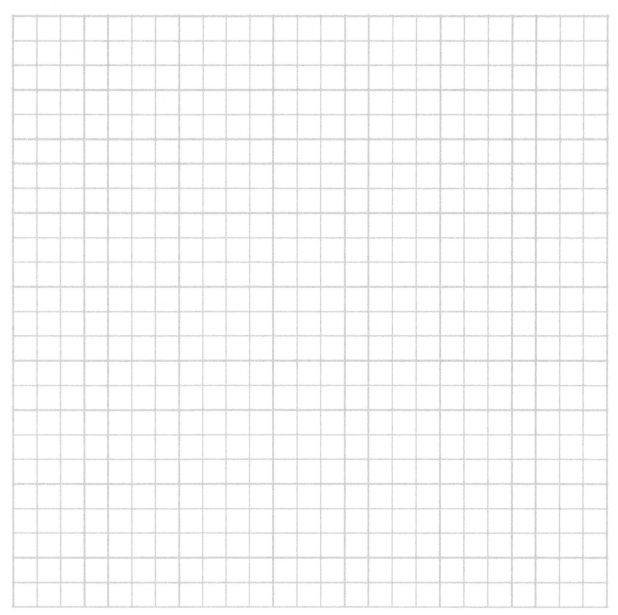

Bedroom 2 Floor Plan

Room Dimensions _____   Window Dimensions_____

Door Dimensions _____   Bed Dimensions _____

Other _____

Bedroom 2 Main Wall Elevation

Wall Dimensions _____   Window Dimensions_____

Bed Dimensions _____   Dresser Dimensions_____

Other _____

Ideas & Inspiration

Bedroom 3 _____

Flooring

Material: _____

Manufacturer: _____

Style/Model Info: _____

_____

Design Pattern: _____

Website: _____

Purchased at: _____

Installed by: _____

Area

L _____ X

W _____

= _____

Add an extra 10% =

_____

Lighting Fixture 1

Manufacturer: _____

Style/Model Info: _____

_____

Website: _____

Purchased at: _____

Installed by: _____

Bulbs

Wattage _____

Type _____

From_____

Changed_____

Lighting Fixture 2

Manufacturer: _____

Style/Model Info: _____

_____

Website: _____

Purchased at: _____

Installed by: _____

Bulbs

Wattage _____

Type _____

From_____

Changed_____

Lighting Fixture 3

Manufacturer: _____

Style/Model Info: _____

_____

Website: _____

Purchased at: _____

Installed by: _____

Bulbs

Wattage _____

Type _____

From_____

Changed_____

Trim Work

Crown Molding

Manufacturer: _____

Style/Model Info: _____

_____

Paint / Stain: _____

Website: _____

Purchased at: _____

Installed by: _____

Linear Footage

Wall 1 _____

Wall 2 _____

Wall 3 _____

Wall 4 _____

Total _____

Floor Molding / Tile Base

Manufacturer: _____

Style/Model Info: _____

_____

Paint / Stain: _____

Website: _____

Purchased at: _____

Installed by: _____

Linear Footage

Wall 1 _____

Wall 2 _____

Wall 3 _____

Wall 4 _____

Total _____

Window / Door Trim

Manufacturer: _____

Style/Model Info: _____

_____

Paint / Stain: _____

Website: _____

Purchased at: _____

Installed by: _____

Linear Footage

Wall 1 _____

Wall 2 _____

Wall 3 _____

Wall 4 _____

Total _____

Wall Covering / Paint 1

Manufacturer: _____

Color: _____

Style/Model Info: _____

_____

Website: _____

Purchased at: _____

Installed by:_____

Area

L _____ X

W _____

= _____

Add an extra 10% =

_____

Wall Covering / Paint 2

Manufacturer: _____

Color: _____

Style/Model Info: _____

_____

Website: _____

Purchased at: _____

Installed by:_____

Area

L _____ X

W _____

= _____

Add an extra 10% =

_____

⊞ Windows

Manufacturer: _____

Style/Model Info: _____

_____

Website: _____

Purchased at: _____

Installed by: _____

Dimensions

W_____

H _____

Type

_____

Material

_____

▓ Window Coverings 1

Manufacturer: _____

Style/Model Info: _____

_____

Rod or Holder: _____

_____

Website: _____

Purchased at: _____

Installed by: _____

Dimensions

L _____

W_____

H _____

Type

_____

Material

_____

Window Coverings 2

Manufacturer: _____

Style/Model Info: _____

_____

Rod or Holder: _____

_____

Website: _____

Purchased at: _____

Installed by: _____

Dimensions

L _____

W_____

H _____

Type

_____

Material

_____

Accessories

_____

_____

_____

_____

_____

_____

_____

_____

_____

_____

_____

_____

_____

_____

Staple Fabric Swatches / Color Chips Here

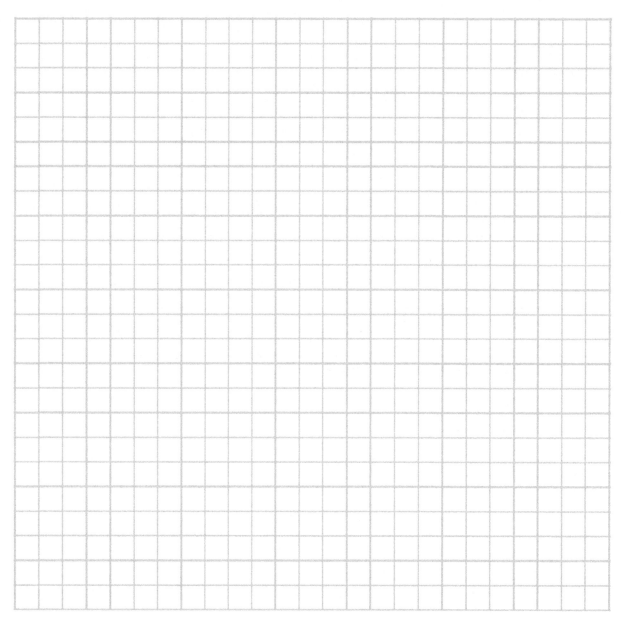

Bedroom 3 Floor Plan

Room Dimensions _____   Window Dimensions_____

Door Dimensions _____   Bed Dimensions _____

Other _____

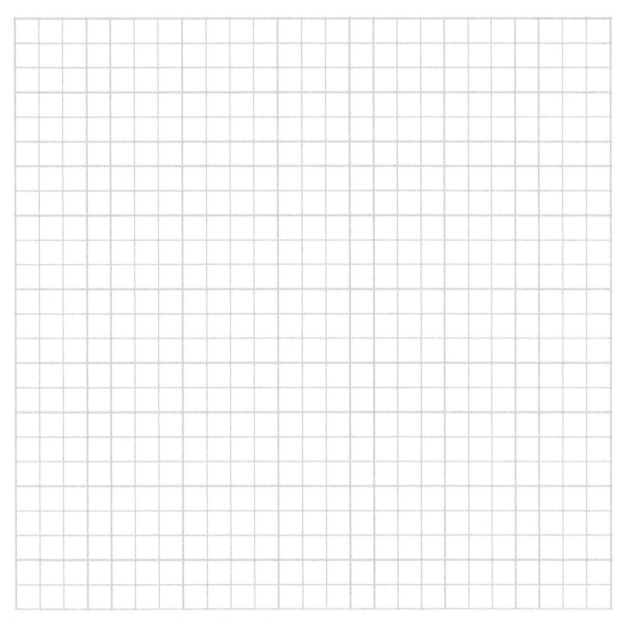

Bedroom 3 Main Wall Elevation

Wall Dimensions _____   Window Dimensions_____

Bed Dimensions _____   Dresser Dimensions_____

Other _____

Ideas & Inspiration

Bedroom 4 _____

Flooring

Material: _____

Manufacturer: _____

Style/Model Info: _____

_____

Design Pattern: _____

Website: _____

Purchased at: _____

Installed by: _____

Area

L _____ X

W _____

= _____

Add an extra 10% =

_____

Lighting Fixture 1

Manufacturer: _____

Style/Model Info: _____

_____

Website: _____

Purchased at: _____

Installed by: _____

Bulbs

Wattage _____

Type _____

From _____

Changed _____

Lighting Fixture 2

Manufacturer: _____

Style/Model Info: _____

_____

Website: _____

Purchased at: _____

Installed by: _____

Bulbs

Wattage _____

Type _____

From _____

Changed _____

Lighting Fixture 3

Manufacturer: _____

Style/Model Info: _____

_____

Website: _____

Purchased at: _____

Installed by: _____

Bulbs

Wattage _____

Type _____

From _____

Changed _____

Trim Work

Crown Molding

Manufacturer: _____

Style/Model Info: _____

_____

Paint / Stain: _____

Website: _____

Purchased at: _____

Installed by: _____

Linear Footage

Wall 1 _____

Wall 2 _____

Wall 3 _____

Wall 4 _____

Total _____

Floor Molding / Tile Base

Manufacturer: _____

Style/Model Info: _____

_____

Paint / Stain: _____

Website: _____

Purchased at: _____

Installed by: _____

Linear Footage

Wall 1 _____

Wall 2 _____

Wall 3 _____

Wall 4 _____

Total _____

Window / Door Trim

Manufacturer: _____

Style/Model Info: _____

_____

Paint / Stain: _____

Website: _____

Purchased at: _____

Installed by: _____

Linear Footage

Wall 1 _____

Wall 2 _____

Wall 3 _____

Wall 4 _____

Total _____

Wall Covering / Paint 1

Manufacturer: _____

Color: _____

Style/Model Info: _____

_____

Website: _____

Purchased at: _____

Installed by: _____

Area

L _____ X

W _____

= _____

Add an extra 10% =

_____

Wall Covering / Paint 2

Manufacturer: _____

Color: _____

Style/Model Info: _____

_____

Website: _____

Purchased at: _____

Installed by: _____

Area

L _____ X

W _____

= _____

Add an extra 10% =

_____

⊞ Windows

Manufacturer: _____

Style/Model Info: _____

_____

Website: _____

Purchased at: _____

Installed by: _____

Dimensions

W_____

H _____

Type
_____

Material
_____

▐▌ Window Coverings 1

Manufacturer: _____

Style/Model Info: _____

_____

Rod or Holder: _____

_____

Website: _____

Purchased at: _____

Installed by: _____

Dimensions

L _____

W_____

H _____

Type
_____

Material
_____

Window Coverings 2

Manufacturer: _____

Style/Model Info: _____

_____

Rod or Holder: _____

_____

Website: _____

Purchased at: _____

Installed by: _____

Dimensions

L _____

W_____

H _____

Type
_____

Material
_____

Accessories

_____

_____

_____

_____

_____

_____

_____

_____

_____

_____

_____

_____

_____

Staple Fabric Swatches / Color Chips Here

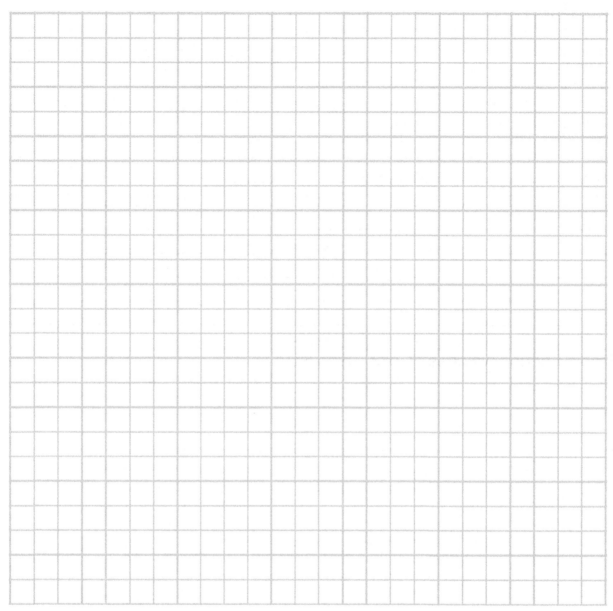

Bedroom 4 Floor Plan

Room Dimensions _____   Window Dimensions_____

Door Dimensions _____   Bed Dimensions _____

Other _____

Bedroom 4 Main Wall Elevation

Wall Dimensions _____   Window Dimensions_____

Bed Dimensions _____   Dresser Dimensions_____

Other _____

Ideas & Inspiration

Bedroom 5 _____

Flooring

Material: _____

Manufacturer: _____

Style/Model Info: _____

_____

Design Pattern: _____

Website: _____

Purchased at: _____

Installed by: _____

Area

L _____ X

W _____

= _____

Add an extra 10% =

_____

Lighting Fixture 1

Manufacturer: _____

Style/Model Info: _____

_____

Website: _____

Purchased at: _____

Installed by: _____

Bulbs

Wattage _____

Type _____

From_____

Changed_____

Lighting Fixture 2

Manufacturer: _____

Style/Model Info: _____

_____

Website: _____

Purchased at: _____

Installed by: _____

Bulbs

Wattage _____

Type _____

From_____

Changed_____

Lighting Fixture 3

Manufacturer: _____

Style/Model Info: _____

_____

Website: _____

Purchased at: _____

Installed by: _____

Bulbs

Wattage _____

Type _____

From_____

Changed_____

Trim Work

Crown Molding

Manufacturer: _____

Style/Model Info: _____

_____

Paint / Stain: _____

Website: _____

Purchased at: _____

Installed by: _____

Linear Footage

Wall 1 _____

Wall 2 _____

Wall 3 _____

Wall 4 _____

Total _____

Floor Molding / Tile Base

Manufacturer: _____

Style/Model Info: _____

_____

Paint / Stain: _____

Website: _____

Purchased at: _____

Installed by: _____

Linear Footage

Wall 1 _____

Wall 2 _____

Wall 3 _____

Wall 4 _____

Total _____

Window / Door Trim

Manufacturer: _____

Style/Model Info: _____

_____

Paint / Stain: _____

Website: _____

Purchased at: _____

Installed by: _____

Linear Footage

Wall 1 _____

Wall 2 _____

Wall 3 _____

Wall 4 _____

Total _____

Wall Covering / Paint 1

Manufacturer: _____

Color: _____

Style/Model Info: _____

_____

Website: _____

Purchased at: _____

Installed by: _____

Area

L _____ X

W _____

= _____

Add an extra 10% =

_____

Wall Covering / Paint 2

Manufacturer: _____

Color: _____

Style/Model Info: _____

_____

Website: _____

Purchased at: _____

Installed by: _____

Area

L _____ X

W _____

= _____

Add an extra 10% =

_____

⊞ Windows

Manufacturer: _____

Style/Model Info: _____

_____

Website: _____

Purchased at: _____

Installed by: _____

Dimensions

W_____

H _____

Type

_____

Material

_____

▌▌ Window Coverings 1

Manufacturer: _____

Style/Model Info: _____

_____

Rod or Holder: _____

_____

Website: _____

Purchased at: _____

Installed by: _____

Dimensions

L _____

W_____

H _____

Type

_____

Material

_____

Window Coverings 2

Manufacturer: _____

Style/Model Info: _____

_____

Rod or Holder: _____

_____

Website: _____

Purchased at: _____

Installed by: _____

Dimensions

L _____

W_____

H _____

Type

_____

Material

_____

Accessories

_____

_____

_____

_____

_____

_____

_____

_____

_____

_____

_____

_____

_____

_____

_____

Staple Fabric Swatches / Color Chips Here

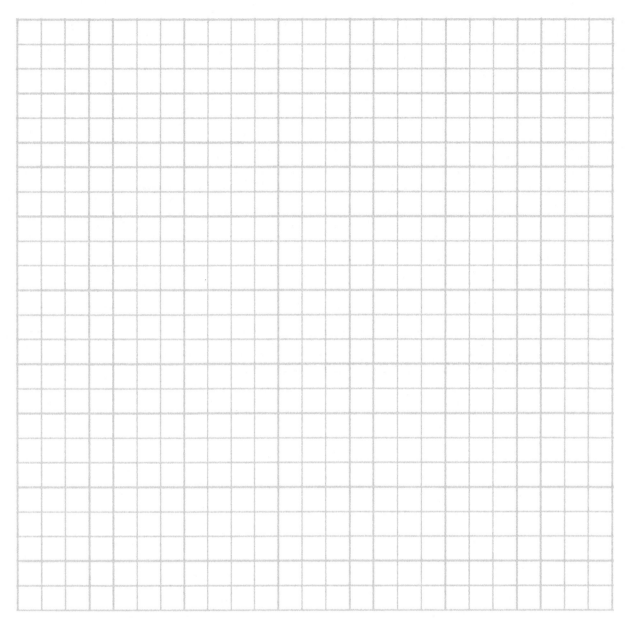

Bedroom 5 Floor Plan

Room Dimensions _____   Window Dimensions_____

Door Dimensions _____   Bed Dimensions _____

Other _____

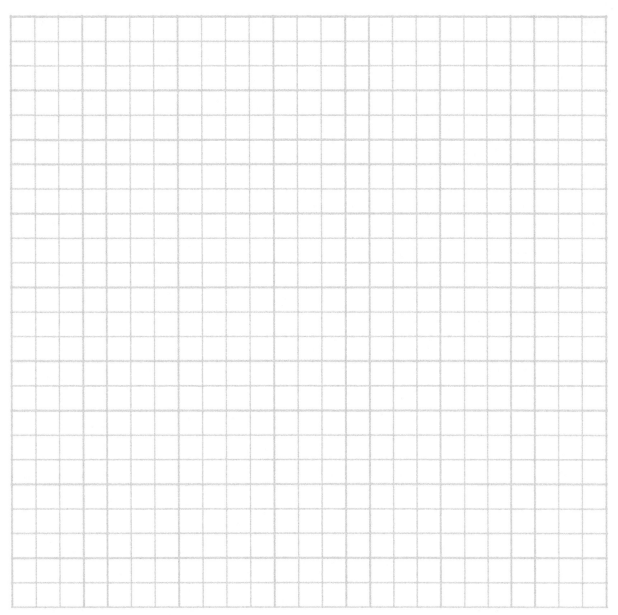

Bedroom 5 Main Wall Elevation

Wall Dimensions _____   Window Dimensions_____

Bed Dimensions _____   Dresser Dimensions_____

Other _____

Ideas & Inspiration

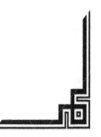

Remodel Checklist (Check those that will be changed and add your own)

Item	Dinning	Kitchen
Appliances		
Dishwasher		
Hood		
Microwave		
Oven		
Refrigerator		
Stove		
Cabinetry		
Backsplash		
Cabinets		
Countertops		
Knobs/Pulls		
Door		
Drywall		
Electrical		
Electrical outlets		
Fan		
GFI outlet		
Lighting		
Switches		
Flooring		
Plaster		

Item	Dining	Kitchen
Plumbing		
Drains		
Faucets		
Pipes		
Gas		
Sink		
Disposal		
Water Filter		
Trim		
Base Moulding		
Crown Moulding		
Door/Window		
Wall Covering		
Window		
Window Covering		

Dining Room

Flooring

Material: _____

Manufacturer: _____

Style/Model Info: _____

_____

Design Pattern: _____

Website: _____

Purchased at: _____

Installed by: _____

Area

L _____ X

W _____

= _____

Add an extra 10% =

_____

Lighting Fixture 1

Manufacturer: _____

Style/Model Info: _____

_____

Website: _____

Purchased at: _____

Installed by: _____

Bulbs

Wattage _____

Type _____

From_____

Changed_____

Lighting Fixture 2

Manufacturer: _____

Style/Model Info: _____

_____

Website: _____

Purchased at: _____

Installed by: _____

Bulbs

Wattage _____

Type _____

From_____

Changed_____

Lighting Fixture 3

Manufacturer: _____

Style/Model Info: _____

_____

Website: _____

Purchased at: _____

Installed by: _____

Bulbs

Wattage _____

Type _____

From _____

Changed _____

Trim Work

Crown Molding

Manufacturer: _____

Style/Model Info: _____

_____

Paint / Stain: _____

Website: _____

Purchased at: _____

Installed by: _____

Linear Footage

Wall 1 _____

Wall 2 _____

Wall 3 _____

Wall 4 _____

Total _____

Floor Molding / Tile Base

Manufacturer: _____

Style/Model Info: _____

_____

Paint / Stain: _____

Website: _____

Purchased at: _____

Installed by: _____

Linear Footage

Wall 1 _____

Wall 2 _____

Wall 3 _____

Wall 4 _____

Total _____

Window / Door Trim

Manufacturer: _____

Style/Model Info: _____

_____

Paint / Stain: _____

Website: _____

Purchased at: _____

Installed by: _____

Linear Footage

Wall 1 _____

Wall 2 _____

Wall 3 _____

Wall 4 _____

Total _____

Wall Covering / Paint 1

Manufacturer: _____

Color: _____

Style/Model Info: _____

_____

Website: _____

Purchased at: _____

Installed by:_____

Area

L _____ X

W _____

= _____

Add an extra 10% =

_____

Wall Covering / Paint 2

Manufacturer: _____

Color: _____

Style/Model Info: _____

_____

Website: _____

Purchased at: _____

Installed by:_____

Area

L _____ X

W _____

= _____

Add an extra 10% =

_____

⊞ Windows

Manufacturer: _____

Style/Model Info: _____

_____

Website: _____

Purchased at: _____

Installed by: _____

Dimensions

W_____

H_____

Type

_____

Material

_____

▓ Window Coverings 1

Manufacturer: _____

Style/Model Info: _____

_____

Rod or Holder: _____

_____

Website: _____

Purchased at: _____

Installed by: _____

Dimensions

L_____

W_____

H_____

Type

_____

Material

_____

Window Coverings 2

Manufacturer: _____

Style/Model Info: _____

_____

Rod or Holder: _____

_____

Website: _____

Purchased at: _____

Installed by: _____

Dimensions

L_____

W_____

H_____

Type

_____

Material

_____

Accessories

_____

_____

_____

_____

_____

_____

_____

_____

_____

_____

_____

_____

_____

_____

Staple Fabric Swatches / Color Chips Here

Dining Room Floor Plan

Room Dimensions _____   Window Dimensions_____

Door Dimensions _____   Table Dimensions _____

Side Board Dimensions _____Other _____

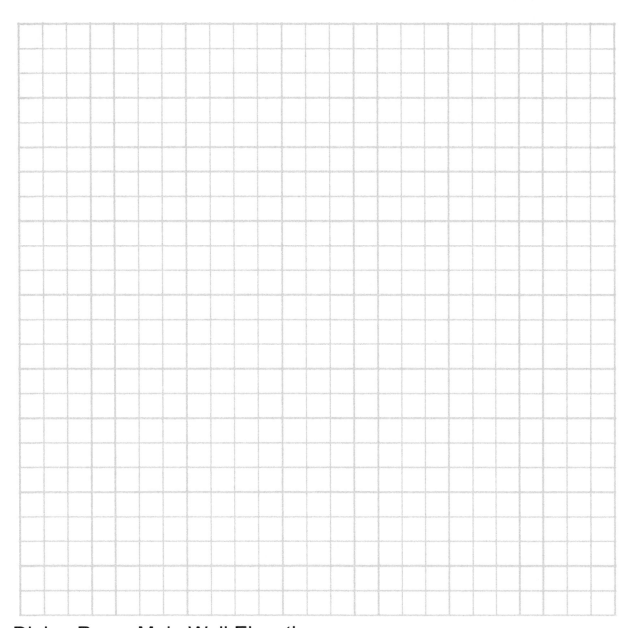

Dining Room Main Wall Elevation

Wall Dimensions _____   Window Dimensions_____

Table Dimensions _____   Side Board Dimensions_____

Other _____

Ideas & Inspiration

Kitchen

 Appliances

Dishwasher

Manufacturer: _____

Style/Model Info: _____

_____

Website: _____

Purchased at: _____

Installed by: _____

Dimensions

D _____

W _____

H _____

Type

_____

Finish _____

Hood

Manufacturer: _____

Style/Model Info: _____

_____

Website: _____

Purchased at: _____

Installed by: _____

Dimensions

D _____

W _____

H _____

Type

_____

Finish _____

Microwave

Manufacturer: _____

Style/Model Info: _____

_____

Website: _____

Purchased at: _____

Installed by: _____

Dimensions

D _____

W _____

H _____

Type

_____

Finish _____

Oven

Manufacturer: _____

Style/Model Info: _____

_____

Gas or Electric: _____

Website: _____

Purchased at: _____

Installed by: _____

Dimensions

D _____

W_____

H _____

Type

_____

Finish_____

Refrigerator

Manufacturer: _____

Style/Model Info: _____

_____

_____

Website: _____

Purchased at: _____

Installed by: _____

Dimensions

D _____

W_____

H _____

Type

_____

Finish_____

Stove / Cooktop

Manufacturer: _____

Style/Model Info: _____

_____

Gas or Electric: _____

Website: _____

Purchased at: _____

Installed by: _____

Dimensions

D _____

W_____

H _____

Type

_____

Finish_____

 # Counters

Backsplash Accent Tile 1

Material: _____

Manufacturer: _____

Style/Model Info: _____

_____

Website: _____

Purchased at: _____

Installed by: _____

Dimensions

L _____

W_____

Thickness _____

Type _____

Material

_____

Backsplash Main Tile

Material: _____

Manufacturer: _____

Style/Model Info: _____

_____

Website: _____

Purchased at: _____

Installed by: _____

Dimensions

L _____

W_____

Thickness _____

Type _____

Material

_____

Cabinetry

Manufacturer: _____

Style/Model Info: _____

_____

Paint or Stain: _____

Website: _____

Purchased at: _____

Installed by: _____

Notes:

(Don't forget to order touch up paint or stain.)

Countertop 1

Material: _____

Manufacturer: _____

Style/Model Info: _____

_____

Website: _____

Purchased at: _____

Installed by: _____

Dimensions

D _____

W_____

H _____

Type

_____

Countertop 2

Material: _____

Manufacturer: _____

Style/Model Info: _____

_____

Website: _____

Purchased at: _____

Installed by: _____

Dimensions

D _____

W_____

H _____

Type

_____

Knobs and Pulls

Material: _____

Manufacturer: _____

Style/Model Info: _____

_____

Website: _____

Purchased at: _____

Installed by: _____

Handle Dimensions

Width _____

Height _____

Center to Center Measurement

_____

Handles _____

Knobs _____

Flooring

Material: _____

Manufacturer: _____

Style/Model Info: _____

_____

Design Pattern: _____

Website: _____

Purchased at: _____

Installed by: _____

Area

L _____ X

W _____

= _____

Add an extra 10% =

_____

Lighting Fixture 1

Manufacturer: _____

Room Location: _____

Style/Model Info: _____

_____

Website: _____

Purchased at: _____

Installed by: _____

Bulbs

Wattage _____

Type _____

From _____

Changed_____

Lighting Fixture 2

Manufacturer: _____

Room Location: _____

Style/Model Info: _____

_____

Website: _____

Purchased at: _____

Installed by: _____

Bulbs

Wattage _____

Type _____

From _____

Changed_____

Lighting Fixture 3

Manufacturer: _____

Room Location: _____

Style/Model Info: _____

_____

Website: _____

Purchased at: _____

Installed by: _____

Bulbs

Wattage _____

Type _____

From _____

Changed _____

Lighting Fixture 4

Manufacturer: _____

Room Location: _____

Style/Model Info: _____

_____

Website: _____

Purchased at: _____

Installed by: _____

Bulbs

Wattage _____

Type _____

From _____

Changed _____

Plumbing Fixtures

Disposal

Manufacturer: _____

Style/Model Info: _____

_____

Website: _____

Purchased at: _____

Installed by: _____

Dimensions

L _____

W _____

Horsepower

_____

Sink

Material: _____

Manufacturer: _____

Style/Model Info: _____

_____

Website: _____

Purchased at: _____

Installed by: _____

Dimensions

L _____

W_____

Faucet Center

_____

Faucet Holes

_____

Material

_____

Sink Faucet

Manufacturer: _____

Style/Model Info: _____

_____

Finish: _____

Website: _____

Purchased at: _____

Installed by: _____

Specifications

# of Holes _____

Spread _____

Mount _____

Water Filter

Manufacturer: _____

Style/Model Info: _____

_____

_____

Website: _____

Purchased at: _____

Installed by: _____

Filtration Method

_____

Replacement filter

_____

Last Changed

_____

≡ Trim Work

Crown Molding

Manufacturer: _____

Style/Model Info: _____

_____

Paint / Stain: _____

Website: _____

Purchased at: _____

Installed by: _____

Linear Footage

Wall 1 _____

Wall 2 _____

Wall 3 _____

Wall 4 _____

Total _____

Floor Molding / Tile Base

Manufacturer: _____

Style/Model Info: _____

_____

Paint / Stain: _____

Website: _____

Purchased at: _____

Installed by: _____

Linear Footage

Wall 1 _____

Wall 2 _____

Wall 3 _____

Wall 4 _____

Total _____

Window / Door Trim

Manufacturer: _____

Style/Model Info: _____

_____

Paint / Stain: _____

Website: _____

Purchased at: _____

Installed by: _____

Linear Footage

Wall 1 _____

Wall 2 _____

Wall 3 _____

Wall 4 _____

Total _____

Wall Covering / Paint 1

Manufacturer: _____

Color: _____

Style/Model Info: _____

_____

Website: _____

Purchased at: _____

Installed by:_____

Area

L _____ X

W _____

= _____

Add an extra 10% =

_____

Wall Covering / Paint 2

Manufacturer: _____

Color: _____

Style/Model Info: _____

_____

Website: _____

Purchased at: _____

Installed by:_____

Area

L _____ X

W _____

= _____

Add an extra 10% =

_____

Windows

Manufacturer: _____

Style/Model Info: _____

_____

_____

Website: _____

Purchased at: _____

Installed by: _____

Dimensions

W_____

H _____

Type

_____

Material

_____

Window Coverings 1

Manufacturer: _____

Style/Model Info: _____

_____

Rod or Holder: _____

_____

Website: _____

Purchased at: _____

Installed by: _____

Dimensions

L _____

W_____

H _____

Type
_____

Material
_____

Window Coverings 2

Manufacturer: _____

Style/Model Info: _____

_____

Rod or Holder: _____

_____

Website: _____

Purchased at: _____

Installed by: _____

Dimensions

L _____

W_____

H _____

Type
_____

Material
_____

_____

Manufacturer: _____

Style/Model Info: _____

_____

Website: _____

Purchased at: _____

Installed by: _____

Notes:

Kitchen

_____

Manufacturer: _____

Style/Model Info: _____

_____

_____

Website: _____

Purchased at: _____

Installed by: _____

_____

Manufacturer: _____

Style/Model Info: _____

_____

_____

Website: _____

Purchased at: _____

Installed by: _____

Notes:

_____

Manufacturer: _____

Style/Model Info: _____

_____

_____

Website: _____

Purchased at: _____

Installed by: _____

Notes:

Accessories

_____

_____

_____

_____

_____

_____

_____

_____

_____

_____

_____

_____

_____

_____

Staple Fabric Swatches / Color Chips Here

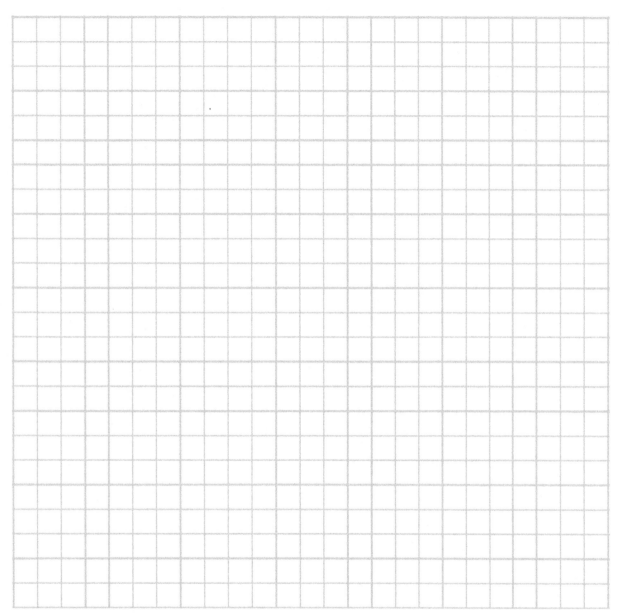

Kitchen Floor Plan

Room Dimensions _____   Window Dimensions_____

Door Dimensions _____   Table Dimensions _____

Side Board Dimensions _____Other _____

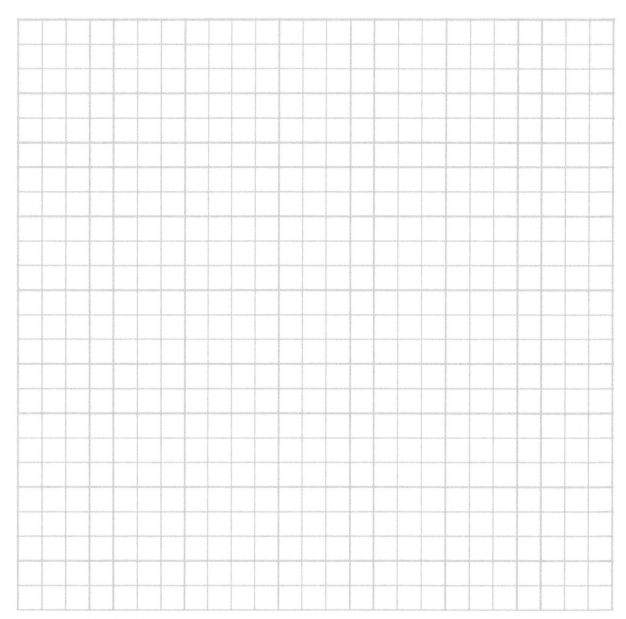

Kitchen Main Wall Elevation

Wall Dimensions _____   Window Dimensions_____

Table Dimensions _____   Side Board Dimensions_____

Other _____

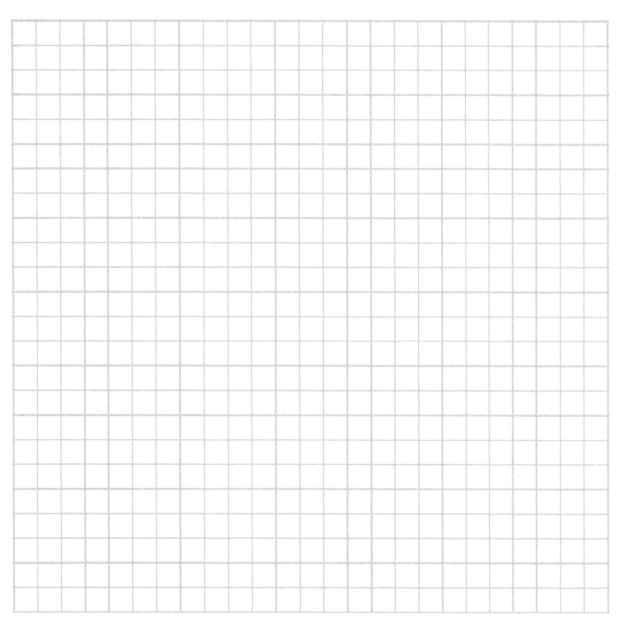

Kitchen Secondary Wall Elevation

Room Dimensions _____ Fridge Dimensions_____

Stove Dimensions _____ Dishwasher _____

Cabinets _____ Sink _____

Ideas & Inspiration

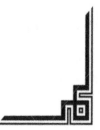

Living Spaces

Remodel Checklist (Check those that will be changed)

Item	Den	Family Room	Home Theater	Living Room
Audio/Visual				
Game System				
Sound				
TV/Screen				
Door				
Drywall				
Electrical				
Electrical outlets				
Fan				
Lighting 1				
Switches				
Dimers				
Flooring				
Storage				
Plaster				
Tile				
Trim				
Base Moulding				
Crown Moulding				
Door/Window				
Wall Covering				
Window				
Window Covering				

Den

Flooring

Material: _____

Manufacturer: _____

Style/Model Info: _____

_____

Design Pattern: _____

Website: _____

Purchased at: _____

Installed by: _____

Area

L _____ X

W _____

= _____

Add an extra 10% =

_____

Lighting Fixture 1

Manufacturer: _____

Style/Model Info: _____

_____

Website: _____

Purchased at: _____

Installed by: _____

Bulbs

Wattage _____

Type _____

From_____

Changed_____

Lighting Fixture 2

Manufacturer: _____

Style/Model Info: _____

_____

Website: _____

Purchased at: _____

Installed by: _____

Bulbs

Wattage _____

Type _____

From_____

Changed_____

Lighting Fixture 3

Manufacturer: _____

Style/Model Info: _____

_____

Website: _____

Purchased at: _____

Installed by: _____

Bulbs

Wattage _____

Type _____

From _____

Changed _____

Trim Work

Crown Molding

Manufacturer: _____

Style/Model Info: _____

_____

Paint / Stain: _____

Website: _____

Purchased at: _____

Installed by: _____

Linear Footage

Wall 1 _____

Wall 2 _____

Wall 3 _____

Wall 4 _____

Total _____

Floor Molding / Tile Base

Manufacturer: _____

Style/Model Info: _____

_____

Paint / Stain: _____

Website: _____

Purchased at: _____

Installed by: _____

Linear Footage

Wall 1 _____

Wall 2 _____

Wall 3 _____

Wall 4 _____

Total _____

Den

Window / Door Trim

Manufacturer: _____

Style/Model Info: _____

_____

Paint / Stain: _____

Website: _____

Purchased at: _____

Installed by: _____

Linear Footage

Wall 1 _____

Wall 2 _____

Wall 3 _____

Wall 4 _____

Total _____

Wall Covering / Paint 1

Manufacturer: _____

Color: _____

Style/Model Info: _____

_____

Website: _____

Purchased at: _____

Installed by:_____

Area

L _____ X

W _____

= _____

Add an extra 10% =

_____

Wall Covering / Paint 2

Manufacturer: _____

Color: _____

Style/Model Info: _____

_____

Website: _____

Purchased at: _____

Installed by:_____

Area

L _____ X

W _____

= _____

Add an extra 10% =

_____

⊞ Windows

Manufacturer: _____

Style/Model Info: _____

_____

Website: _____

Purchased at: _____

Installed by: _____

Dimensions

W_____

H _____

Type
_____

Material
_____

▐▌ Window Coverings 1

Manufacturer: _____

Style/Model Info: _____

_____

Rod or Holder: _____

_____

Website: _____

Purchased at: _____

Installed by: _____

Dimensions

L _____

W_____

H _____

Type
_____

Material
_____

Window Coverings 2

Manufacturer: _____

Style/Model Info: _____

_____

Rod or Holder: _____

_____

Website: _____

Purchased at: _____

Installed by: _____

Dimensions

L _____

W_____

H _____

Type
_____

Material
_____

Accessories

_____

_____

_____

_____

_____

_____

_____

_____

_____

_____

_____

_____

_____

_____

Staple Fabric Swatches / Color Chips Here

Den

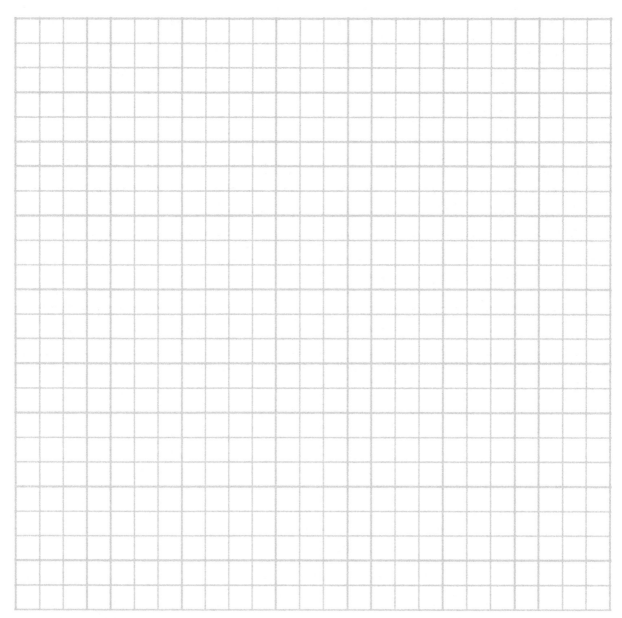

Den Floor Plan

Room Dimensions _____ Window Dimensions_____

Door Dimensions _____ Couch Dimensions _____

Coffee table _____ Other Seating _____

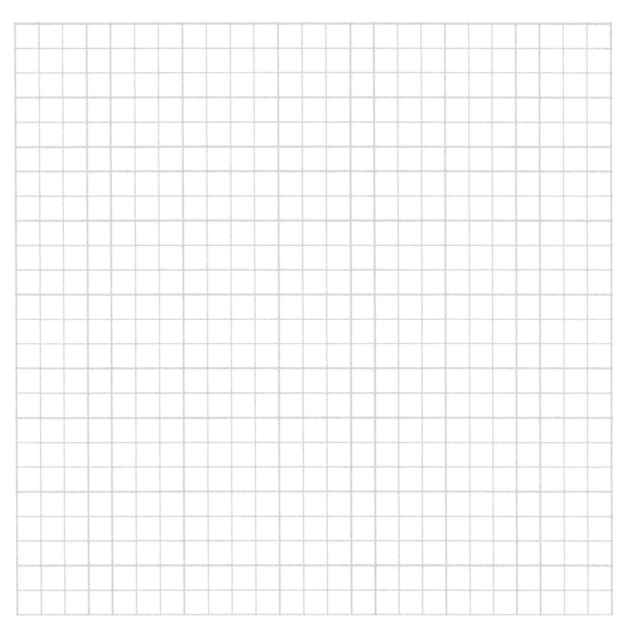

Den Main Wall Elevation

Wall Dimensions _____   Window Dimensions_____

Couch Dimensions _____   Other Dimensions_____

Other _____

Ideas & Inspiration

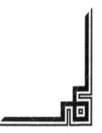

Family Room

Flooring

Material: _____

Manufacturer: _____

Style/Model Info: _____

_____

Design Pattern: _____

Website: _____

Purchased at: _____

Installed by: _____

Area

L _____ X

W _____

= _____

Add an extra 10% =

_____

Lighting Fixture 1

Manufacturer: _____

Style/Model Info: _____

_____

Website: _____

Purchased at: _____

Installed by: _____

Bulbs

Wattage _____

Type _____

From_____

Changed_____

Lighting Fixture 2

Manufacturer: _____

Style/Model Info: _____

_____

Website: _____

Purchased at: _____

Installed by: _____

Bulbs

Wattage _____

Type _____

From_____

Changed_____

Lighting Fixture 3

Manufacturer: _____

Style/Model Info: _____

_____

Website: _____

Purchased at: _____

Installed by: _____

Bulbs

Wattage _____

Type _____

From _____

Changed _____

▬ Trim Work

Crown Molding

Manufacturer: _____

Style/Model Info: _____

_____

Paint / Stain: _____

Website: _____

Purchased at: _____

Installed by: _____

Linear Footage

Wall 1 _____

Wall 2 _____

Wall 3 _____

Wall 4 _____

Total _____

Floor Molding / Tile Base

Manufacturer: _____

Style/Model Info: _____

_____

Paint / Stain: _____

Website: _____

Purchased at: _____

Installed by: _____

Linear Footage

Wall 1 _____

Wall 2 _____

Wall 3 _____

Wall 4 _____

Total _____

Window / Door Trim

Manufacturer: _____

Style/Model Info: _____

_____

Paint / Stain: _____

Website: _____

Purchased at: _____

Installed by: _____

Linear Footage

Wall 1 _____

Wall 2 _____

Wall 3 _____

Wall 4 _____

Total _____

Wall Covering / Paint 1

Manufacturer: _____

Color: _____

Style/Model Info: _____

_____

Website: _____

Purchased at: _____

Installed by: _____

Area

L _____ X

W _____

= _____

Add an extra 10% =

_____

Wall Covering / Paint 2

Manufacturer: _____

Color: _____

Style/Model Info: _____

_____

Website: _____

Purchased at: _____

Installed by: _____

Area

L _____ X

W _____

= _____

Add an extra 10% =

_____

⊞ Windows

Manufacturer: _____

Style/Model Info: _____

_____

Website: _____

Purchased at: _____

Installed by: _____

Dimensions

W_____

H _____

Type

_____

Material

_____

▮ Window Coverings 1

Manufacturer: _____

Style/Model Info: _____

_____

Rod or Holder: _____

_____

Website: _____

Purchased at: _____

Installed by: _____

Dimensions

L _____

W_____

H _____

Type

_____

Material

_____

Window Coverings 2

Manufacturer: _____

Style/Model Info: _____

_____

Rod or Holder: _____

_____

Website: _____

Purchased at: _____

Installed by: _____

Dimensions

L _____

W_____

H _____

Type

_____

Material

_____

Accessories

_____

_____

_____

_____

_____

_____

_____

_____

_____

_____

_____

_____

_____

_____

Staple Fabric Swatches / Color Chips Here

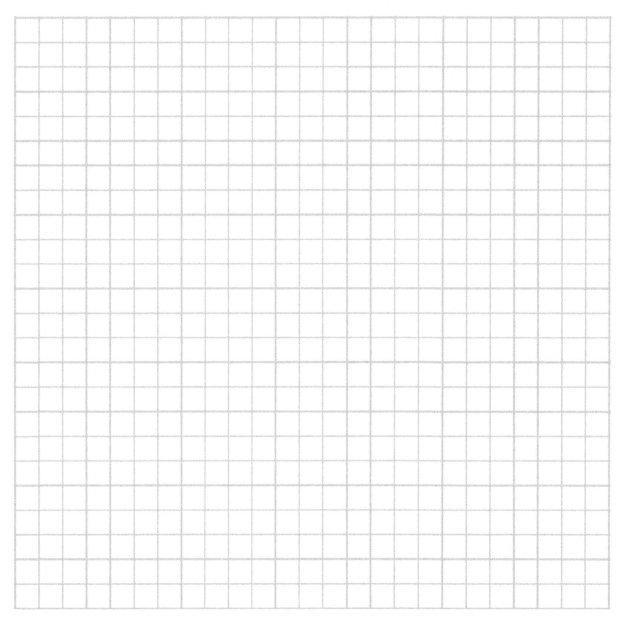

Family Room Floor Plan

Room Dimensions _____   Window Dimensions_____

Door Dimensions _____   Couch Dimensions _____

Coffee table _____   Other Seating _____

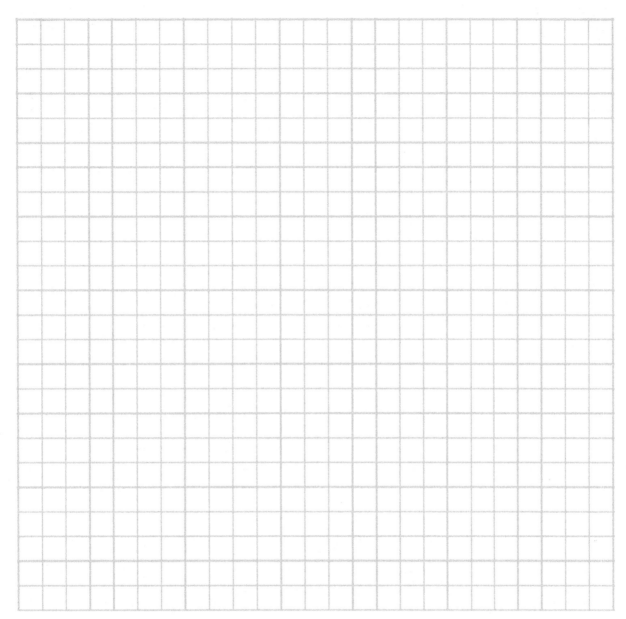

Family Room Main Wall Elevation

Wall Dimensions _____   Window Dimensions_____

Couch Dimensions _____   Other Dimensions_____

Other _____

Ideas & Inspiration

Home Theater

Audio / Visual

Television / Screen

Manufacturer: _____

Style/Model Info: _____

_____

Mount: _____

Website: _____

Purchased at: _____

Installed by: _____

Notes

Sound System

Manufacturer: _____

Style/Model Info: _____

_____

Website: _____

Purchased at: _____

Installed by: _____

Notes

Game System

Manufacturer: _____

Style/Model Info: _____

_____

Website: _____

Purchased at: _____

Installed by: _____

Notes

_____

Manufacturer: _____

Style/Model Info: _____

_____

_____

Website: _____

Purchased at: _____

Installed by: _____

Notes

_____

Manufacturer: _____

Style/Model Info: _____

_____

_____

Website: _____

Purchased at: _____

Installed by: _____

Notes

_____

Manufacturer: _____

Style/Model Info: _____

_____

_____

Website: _____

Purchased at: _____

Installed by: _____

Notes

Flooring

Material: _____

Manufacturer: _____

Style/Model Info: _____

_____

Design Pattern: _____

Website: _____

Purchased at: _____

Installed by: _____

Area

L _____ X

W _____

= _____

Add an extra 10% =

_____

Lighting

Lighting Fixture 1

Manufacturer: _____

Style/Model Info: _____

_____

Website: _____

Purchased at: _____

Installed by: _____

Bulbs

Wattage _____

Type _____

From _____

Changed _____

Lighting Fixture 2

Manufacturer: _____

Style/Model Info: _____

_____

Website: _____

Purchased at: _____

Installed by: _____

Bulbs

Wattage _____

Type _____

From _____

Changed _____

Lighting Fixture 3

Manufacturer: _____

Style/Model Info: _____

_____

Website: _____

Purchased at: _____

Installed by: _____

Bulbs

Wattage _____

Type _____

From_____

Changed_____

▥ Trim Work

Crown Molding

Manufacturer: _____

Style/Model Info: _____

_____

Paint / Stain: _____

Website: _____

Purchased at: _____

Installed by: _____

Linear Footage

Wall 1 _____

Wall 2 _____

Wall 3 _____

Wall 4 _____

Total _____

Floor Molding / Tile Base

Manufacturer: _____

Style/Model Info: _____

_____

Paint / Stain: _____

Website: _____

Purchased at: _____

Installed by: _____

Linear Footage

Wall 1 _____

Wall 2 _____

Wall 3 _____

Wall 4 _____

Total _____

Window / Door Trim

Manufacturer: _____

Style/Model Info: _____

_____

Paint / Stain: _____

Website: _____

Purchased at: _____

Installed by: _____

Linear Footage

Wall 1 _____

Wall 2 _____

Wall 3 _____

Wall 4 _____

Total _____

Wall Covering / Paint 1

Manufacturer: _____

Color: _____

Style/Model Info: _____

_____

Website: _____

Purchased at: _____

Installed by:_____

Area

L _____ X

W _____

= _____

Add an extra 10% =

_____

Wall Covering / Paint 2

Manufacturer: _____

Color: _____

Style/Model Info: _____

_____

Website: _____

Purchased at: _____

Installed by:_____

Area

L _____ X

W _____

= _____

Add an extra 10% =

_____

⊞ Windows

Manufacturer: _____

Style/Model Info: _____

_____

Website: _____

Purchased at: _____

Installed by: _____

Dimensions

W_____

H _____

Type
_____

Material
_____

▐▌ Window Coverings 1

Manufacturer: _____

Style/Model Info: _____

_____

Rod or Holder: _____

_____

Website: _____

Purchased at: _____

Installed by: _____

Dimensions

L _____

W_____

H _____

Type
_____

Material
_____

Window Coverings 2

Manufacturer: _____

Style/Model Info: _____

_____

Rod or Holder: _____

_____

Website: _____

Purchased at: _____

Installed by: _____

Dimensions

L _____

W_____

H _____

Type
_____

Material
_____

_____

Manufacturer: _____

Style/Model Info: _____

_____

_____

Website: _____

Purchased at: _____

Installed by: _____

_____

Manufacturer: _____

Style/Model Info: _____

_____

_____

Website: _____

Purchased at: _____

Installed by: _____

Notes

_____

Manufacturer: _____

Style/Model Info: _____

_____

_____

Website: _____

Purchased at: _____

Installed by: _____

Notes

Accessories

_____

_____

_____

_____

_____

_____

_____

_____

_____

_____

_____

_____

_____

Staple Fabric Swatches / Color Chips Here

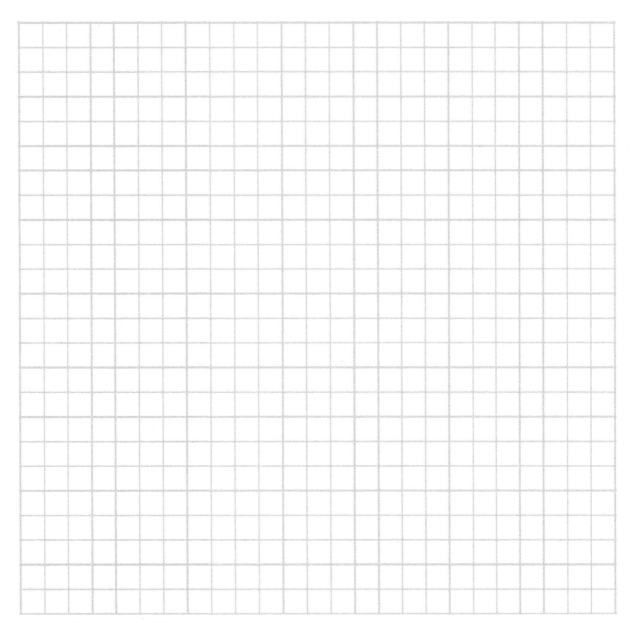

Home Theater Floor Plan

Room Dimensions _____   Window Dimensions_____

Door Dimensions _____   Couch Dimensions _____

Coffee table _____   Entertainment Center _____

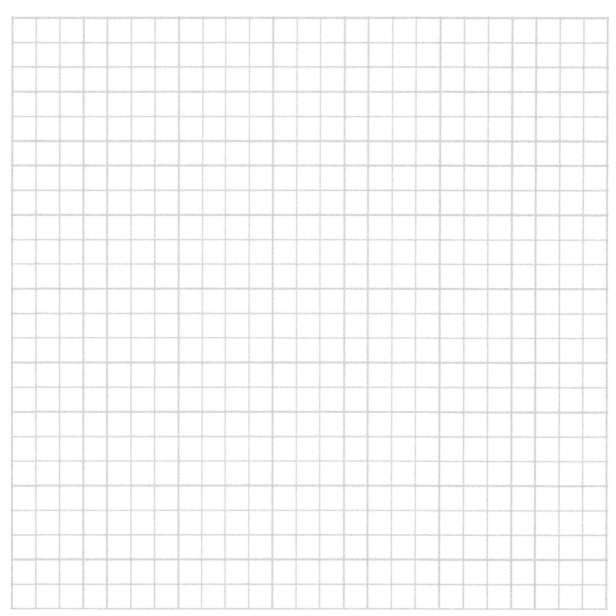

Home Theater Main Wall Elevation

Wall Dimensions _____   Window Dimensions_____

Entertainment Center Dimensions _____ Other Dimensions_____

Other _____

Ideas & Inspiration

Living Room

Flooring

Material: _____

Manufacturer: _____

Style/Model Info: _____

_____

Design Pattern: _____

Website: _____

Purchased at: _____

Installed by: _____

Area

L _____ X

W _____

= _____

Add an extra 10% =

_____

Lighting Fixture 1

Manufacturer: _____

Style/Model Info: _____

_____

Website: _____

Purchased at: _____

Installed by: _____

Bulbs

Wattage _____

Type _____

From_____

Changed_____

Lighting Fixture 2

Manufacturer: _____

Style/Model Info: _____

_____

Website: _____

Purchased at: _____

Installed by: _____

Bulbs

Wattage _____

Type _____

From_____

Changed_____

Lighting Fixture 3

Manufacturer: _____

Style/Model Info: _____

_____

Website: _____

Purchased at: _____

Installed by: _____

Bulbs

Wattage _____

Type _____

From_____

Changed_____

Trim Work

Crown Molding

Manufacturer: _____

Style/Model Info: _____

_____

Paint / Stain: _____

Website: _____

Purchased at: _____

Installed by: _____

Linear Footage

Wall 1 _____

Wall 2 _____

Wall 3 _____

Wall 4 _____

Total _____

Floor Molding / Tile Base

Manufacturer: _____

Style/Model Info: _____

_____

Paint / Stain: _____

Website: _____

Purchased at: _____

Installed by: _____

Linear Footage

Wall 1 _____

Wall 2 _____

Wall 3 _____

Wall 4 _____

Total _____

Window / Door Trim

Manufacturer: _____

Style/Model Info: _____

_____

Paint / Stain: _____

Website: _____

Purchased at: _____

Installed by: _____

Linear Footage

Wall 1 _____

Wall 2 _____

Wall 3 _____

Wall 4 _____

Total _____

Wall Covering / Paint 1

Manufacturer: _____

Color: _____

Style/Model Info: _____

_____

Website: _____

Purchased at: _____

Installed by:_____

Area

L _____ X

W _____

= _____

Add an extra 10% =

_____

Wall Covering / Paint 2

Manufacturer: _____

Color: _____

Style/Model Info: _____

_____

Website: _____

Purchased at: _____

Installed by:_____

Area

L _____ X

W _____

= _____

Add an extra 10% =

_____

⊞ Windows

Manufacturer: _____

Style/Model Info: _____

_____

Website: _____

Purchased at: _____

Installed by: _____

Dimensions

W_____

H _____

Type

_____

Material

_____

▒ Window Coverings 1

Manufacturer: _____

Style/Model Info: _____

_____

Rod or Holder: _____

_____

Website: _____

Purchased at: _____

Installed by: _____

Dimensions

L _____

W_____

H _____

Type

_____

Material

_____

Window Coverings 2

Manufacturer: _____

Style/Model Info: _____

_____

Rod or Holder: _____

_____

Website: _____

Purchased at: _____

Installed by: _____

Dimensions

L _____

W_____

H _____

Type

_____

Material

_____

Accessories

_____

_____

_____

_____

_____

_____

_____

_____

_____

_____

_____

_____

_____

_____

Staple Fabric Swatches / Color Chips Here

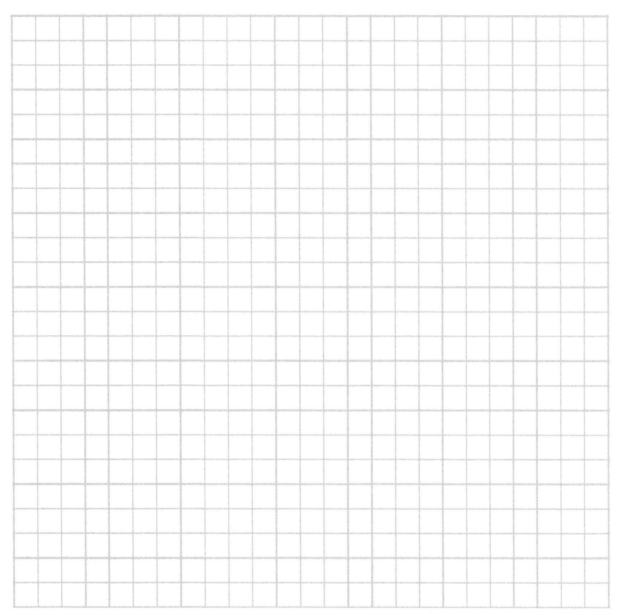

Living Room Floor Plan

Room Dimensions _____   Window Dimensions_____

Door Dimensions _____   Couch Dimensions _____

Coffee table _____   Other Seating _____

Living Room Main Wall Elevation

Wall Dimensions _____   Window Dimensions_____

Couch Dimensions _____   Other Dimensions_____

Other _____

Ideas & Inspiration

Working Spaces

Remodel Checklist (Check those that will be changed and add your own)

Item	Office	Laundry	Walk-in Closet
Door			
Drywall			
Electrical			
Electrical outlets			
Fan			
Lighting			
Switches			
Timers			
Flooring			
Office Equipment			
Plaster			
Plumbing			
Sink			
Storage			
Tile			
Trim			
Base Moulding			
Crown Moulding			
Door/Window			
Wall Covering			
Washer/Dryer			
Window			
Window Covering			

Home Office

Cabinetry/ Storage

Manufacturer: _____

Style/Model Info: _____

_____

Website: _____

Purchased at: _____

Installed by: _____

Dimensions

D _____

W_____

H _____

Type

_____

Material

_____

Desk

Manufacturer: _____

Style/Model Info: _____

_____

Website: _____

Purchased at: _____

Installed by: _____

Dimensions

D _____

W_____

H _____

Type

_____

Material

_____

Knobs and Pulls

Material: _____

Manufacturer: _____

Style/Model Info: _____

_____

Website: _____

Purchased at: _____

Installed by: _____

Handle Dimensions

Width _____

Height _____

Center to Center Measurement

_____

Handles _____

Knobs _____

Flooring

Material: _____

Manufacturer: _____

Style/Model Info: _____

_____

Design Pattern: _____

Website: _____

Purchased at: _____

Installed by: _____

Area

L _____ X

W _____

= _____

Add an extra 10% =

_____

Lighting Fixture 1

Manufacturer: _____

Style/Model Info: _____

_____

_____

Website: _____

Purchased at: _____

Installed by: _____

Bulbs

Wattage _____

Type _____

From_____

Changed_____

Lighting Fixture 2

Manufacturer: _____

Style/Model Info: _____

_____

Website: _____

Purchased at: _____

Installed by: _____

Bulbs

Wattage _____

Type _____

From_____

Changed_____

Lighting Fixture 3

Manufacturer: _____

Style/Model Info: _____

_____

Website: _____

Purchased at: _____

Installed by: _____

Bulbs

Wattage _____

Type _____

From _____

Changed _____

Technical Components

_____

Manufacturer: _____

Style/Model Info: _____

_____

_____

Website: _____

Purchased at: _____

Installed by: _____

Notes

_____

Manufacturer: _____

Style/Model Info: _____

_____

_____

Website: _____

Purchased at: _____

Installed by: _____

Notes

_____

Manufacturer: _____

Style/Model Info: _____

_____

_____

Website: _____

Purchased at: _____

Installed by: _____

_____

Manufacturer: _____

Style/Model Info: _____

_____

_____

Website: _____

Purchased at: _____

Installed by: _____

_____

Manufacturer: _____

Style/Model Info: _____

_____

_____

Website: _____

Purchased at: _____

Installed by: _____

_____

Manufacturer: _____

Style/Model Info: _____

_____

_____

Website: _____

Purchased at: _____

Installed by: _____

Notes

Trim Work

Crown Molding

Manufacturer: _____

Style/Model Info: _____

_____

Paint / Stain: _____

Website: _____

Purchased at: _____

Installed by: _____

Linear Footage

Wall 1 _____

Wall 2 _____

Wall 3 _____

Wall 4 _____

Total _____

Floor Molding / Tile Base

Manufacturer: _____

Style/Model Info: _____

_____

Paint / Stain: _____

Website: _____

Purchased at: _____

Installed by: _____

Linear Footage

Wall 1 _____

Wall 2 _____

Wall 3 _____

Wall 4 _____

Total _____

Window / Door Trim

Manufacturer: _____

Style/Model Info: _____

_____

Paint / Stain: _____

Website: _____

Purchased at: _____

Installed by: _____

Linear Footage

Wall 1 _____

Wall 2 _____

Wall 3 _____

Wall 4 _____

Total _____

Wall Covering / Paint 1

Manufacturer: _____

Color: _____

Style/Model Info: _____

_____

Website: _____

Purchased at: _____

Installed by:_____

Area

L _____ X

W _____

= _____

Add an extra 10% =

_____

Wall Covering / Paint 2

Manufacturer: _____

Color: _____

Style/Model Info: _____

_____

Website: _____

Purchased at: _____

Installed by:_____

Area

L _____ X

W _____

= _____

Add an extra 10% =

_____

⊞ Windows

Manufacturer: _____

Style/Model Info: _____

_____

Website: _____

Purchased at: _____

Installed by: _____

Dimensions

W_____

H _____

Type

_____

Material

_____

▥ Window Coverings 1

Manufacturer: _____

Style/Model Info: _____

_____

Rod or Holder: _____

_____

Website: _____

Purchased at: _____

Installed by: _____

Dimensions

L _____

W_____

H _____

Type

_____

Material

_____

Window Coverings 2

Manufacturer: _____

Style/Model Info: _____

_____

Rod or Holder: _____

_____

Website: _____

Purchased at: _____

Installed by: _____

Dimensions

L _____

W_____

H _____

Type

_____

Material

_____

Accessories

_____

_____

_____

_____

_____

_____

_____

_____

_____

_____

_____

_____

_____

Staple Fabric Swatches / Color Chips Here

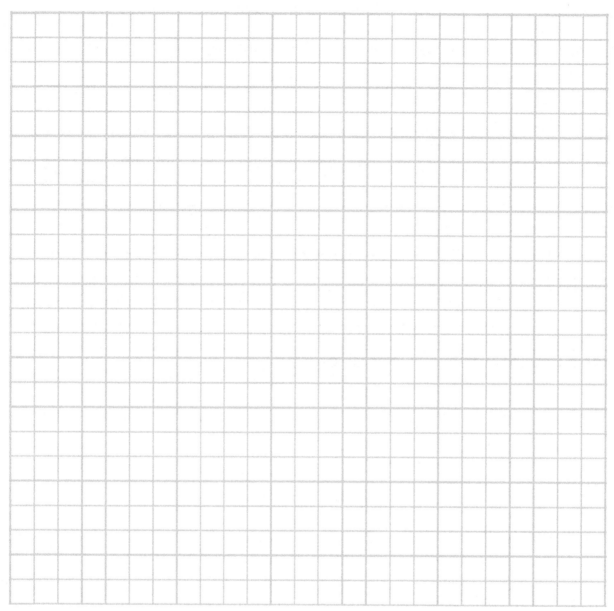

Office Floor Plan

Room Dimensions _____   Window Dimensions_____

Door Dimensions _____   Storage Dimensions _____

Desk Dimensions _____   Other _____

Office Main Wall Elevation

Wall Dimensions _____   Window Dimensions_____

Storage Dimensions _____   Desk Dimensions _____

Other _____

Ideas & Inspiration

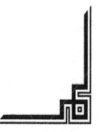

Laundry Room

Washing Machine

Manufacturer: _____

Style/Model Info: _____

_____

Website: _____

Purchased at: _____

Installed by: _____

Dimensions

D _____

W _____

H _____

Type
_____

Material
_____

Dryer

Manufacturer: _____

Style/Model Info: _____

_____

Website: _____

Purchased at: _____

Installed by: _____

Dimensions

D _____

W _____

H _____

Type
_____

Material
_____

Cabinetry / Storage

Manufacturer: _____

Style/Model Info: _____

_____

Paint / Stain: _____

Website: _____

Purchased at: _____

Installed by: _____

Dimensions

D _____

W _____

H _____

Type
_____

Material
_____

Fan

Manufacturer: _____

Style/Model Info: _____

_____

Website: _____

Purchased at: _____

Installed by: _____

Specs:

Voltage:_____

Light: yes   no

Bulb type: _____

Wattage: _____

Flooring

Material: _____

Manufacturer: _____

Style/Model Info: _____

_____

Design Pattern: _____

Website: _____

Purchased at: _____

Installed by: _____

Area

L _____ X

W _____

= _____

Add an extra 10% =

_____

Lighting Fixture 1

Manufacturer: _____

Style/Model Info: _____

_____

Website: _____

Purchased at: _____

Installed by: _____

Bulbs

Wattage _____

Type _____

From_____

Changed_____

Lighting Fixture 2

Manufacturer: _____

Style/Model Info: _____

_____

Website: _____

Purchased at: _____

Installed by: _____

Bulbs

Wattage _____

Type _____

From _____

Changed _____

Sink / Laundry Basin

Material: _____

Manufacturer: _____

Style/Model Info: _____

_____

Website: _____

Purchased at: _____

Installed by: _____

Dimensions

L _____

W _____

Faucet Center

_____

Faucet Holes

_____

Material

_____

Sink Faucet

Manufacturer: _____

Style/Model Info: _____

_____

Finish: _____

Website: _____

Purchased at: _____

Installed by: _____

Specifications

# of Holes _____

Spread _____

Mount _____

Trim Work

Crown Molding

Manufacturer: _____

Style/Model Info: _____

_____

Paint / Stain: _____

Website: _____

Purchased at: _____

Installed by: _____

Linear Footage

Wall 1 _____

Wall 2 _____

Wall 3 _____

Wall 4 _____

Total _____

Floor Molding / Tile Base

Manufacturer: _____

Style/Model Info: _____

_____

Paint / Stain: _____

Website: _____

Purchased at: _____

Installed by: _____

Linear Footage

Wall 1 _____

Wall 2 _____

Wall 3 _____

Wall 4 _____

Total _____

Window / Door Trim

Manufacturer: _____

Style/Model Info: _____

_____

Paint / Stain: _____

Website: _____

Purchased at: _____

Installed by: _____

Linear Footage

Wall 1 _____

Wall 2 _____

Wall 3 _____

Wall 4 _____

Total _____

Wall Covering / Paint 1

Manufacturer: _____

Color: _____

Style/Model Info: _____

_____

Website: _____

Purchased at: _____

Installed by:_____

Area

L _____ X

W _____

= _____

Add an extra 10% =

_____

Wall Covering / Paint 2

Manufacturer: _____

Color: _____

Style/Model Info: _____

_____

Website: _____

Purchased at: _____

Installed by:_____

Area

L _____ X

W _____

= _____

Add an extra 10% =

_____

Windows

Manufacturer: _____

Style/Model Info: _____

_____

_____

Website: _____

Purchased at: _____

Installed by: _____

Dimensions

W_____

H _____

Type

_____

Material

_____

Window Coverings 1

Manufacturer: _____

Style/Model Info: _____

_____

Rod or Holder: _____

_____

Website: _____

Purchased at: _____

Installed by: _____

Dimensions

L _____

W_____

H _____

Type

_____

Material

_____

Window Coverings 2

Manufacturer: _____

Style/Model Info: _____

_____

Rod or Holder: _____

_____

Website: _____

Purchased at: _____

Installed by: _____

Dimensions

L _____

W_____

H _____

Type

_____

Material

_____

_____

Manufacturer: _____

Style/Model Info: _____

_____

Website: _____

Purchased at: _____

Installed by: _____

Notes

Accessories

_____

_____

_____

_____

_____

_____

_____

_____

_____

_____

_____

_____

_____

Staple Fabric Swatches / Color Chips Here

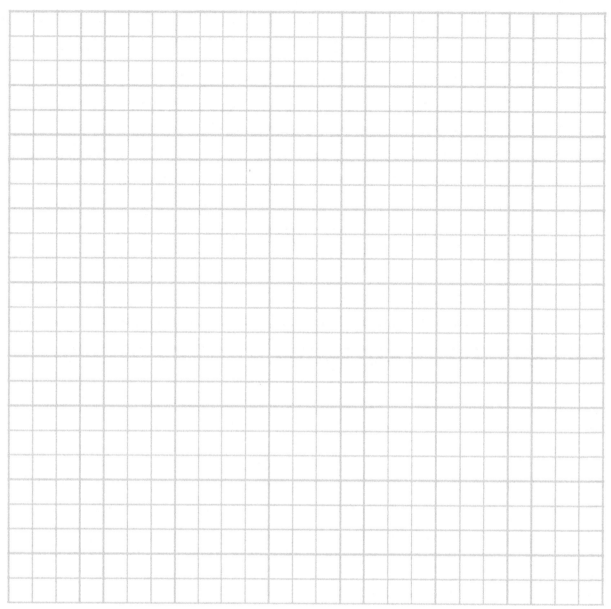

Laundry Room Floor Plan

Room Dimensions _____   Window Dimensions_____

Door Dimensions _____   Storage Dimensions _____

Washer Dimensions _____   Dryer Dimensions _____

Laundry Room Main Wall Elevation

Wall Dimensions _____   Window Dimensions_____

Storage Dimensions _____   Other _____

Washer Dimensions _____   Dryer Dimensions _____

Ideas & Inspiration

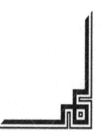

Walk-in Closet

Cabinetry / Storage

Manufacturer: _____

Style/Model Info: _____

_____

Paint / Stain: _____

Website: _____

Purchased at: _____

Installed by: _____

Dimensions

D _____

W_____

H _____

Type

_____

Material

_____

Flooring

Material: _____

Manufacturer: _____

Style/Model Info: _____

_____

Website: _____

Purchased at: _____

Installed by: _____

Area

L _____ X

W_____

= _____

Add an extra 10% =

_____

Lighting Fixture 1

Manufacturer: _____

Style/Model Info: _____

_____

Website: _____

Purchased at: _____

Installed by: _____

Bulbs

Wattage _____

Type _____

From_____

Changed_____

≡ Trim Work

Crown Molding

Manufacturer: _____

Style/Model Info: _____

_____

Paint / Stain: _____

Website: _____

Purchased at: _____

Installed by: _____

Linear Footage

Wall 1 _____

Wall 2 _____

Wall 3 _____

Wall 4 _____

Total _____

Floor Molding / Tile Base

Manufacturer: _____

Style/Model Info: _____

_____

Paint / Stain: _____

Website: _____

Purchased at: _____

Installed by: _____

Linear Footage

Wall 1 _____

Wall 2 _____

Wall 3 _____

Wall 4 _____

Total _____

Window / Door Trim

Manufacturer: _____

Style/Model Info: _____

_____

Paint / Stain: _____

Website: _____

Purchased at: _____

Installed by: _____

Linear Footage

Wall 1 _____

Wall 2 _____

Wall 3 _____

Wall 4 _____

Total _____

Wall Covering / Paint 1

Manufacturer: _____

Color: _____

Style/Model Info: _____

_____

Website: _____

Purchased at: _____

Installed by: _____

Area

L _____ X

W _____

= _____

Add an extra 10% =

_____

Wall Covering / Paint 2

Manufacturer: _____

Color: _____

Style/Model Info: _____

_____

Website: _____

Purchased at: _____

Installed by: _____

Area

L _____ X

W _____

= _____

Add an extra 10% =

_____

Windows

Manufacturer: _____

Style/Model Info: _____

_____

_____

Website: _____

Purchased at: _____

Installed by: _____

Dimensions

W_____

H _____

Type

_____

Material

_____

Window Coverings 1

Manufacturer: _____

Style/Model Info: _____

_____

Rod or Holder: _____

_____

Website: _____

Purchased at: _____

Installed by: _____

Dimensions

L _____

W _____

H _____

Type
_____

Material
_____

Window Coverings 2

Manufacturer: _____

Style/Model Info: _____

_____

Rod or Holder: _____

_____

Website: _____

Purchased at: _____

Installed by: _____

Dimensions

L _____

W _____

H _____

Type
_____

Material
_____

_____

Manufacturer: _____

Style/Model Info: _____

_____

Website: _____

Purchased at: _____

Installed by: _____

Notes

Accessories

_____

_____

_____

_____

_____

_____

_____

_____

_____

_____

_____

_____

_____

_____

Staple Fabric Swatches / Color Chips Here

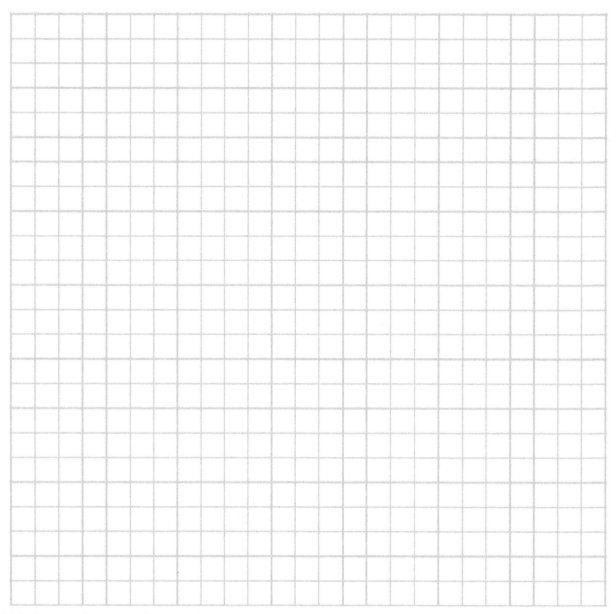

Walk-in Closet Floor Plan

Room Dimensions _____   Window Dimensions_____

Door Dimensions _____   Storage Dimensions _____

Other _____

Walk-in Closet Main Wall Elevation

Wall Dimensions _____   Window Dimensions_____

Storage Dimensions _____   Other _____

Ideas & Inspiration

Notes:

Made in the USA
Columbia, SC
28 October 2018